THE RED ISLAND

Graeme Sparkes was born in Launceston, Tasmania. He has taught in high schools, picked tobacco, driven taxis and travelled in Latin America, Europe, the United States and Australia.

BY THE SAME AUTHOR

Beyond Tijuana:
A Journey through Latin America

the red island

a journey around australia

graeme sparkes

THE TEXT PUBLISHING COMPANY
MELBOURNE AUSTRALIA

The Text Publishing Company
171 La Trobe Street
Melbourne Victoria 3000
Australia

Copyright © Graeme Sparkes
1997

All rights reserved. Without
limiting the rights under
copyright above, no part of this
publication shall be
reproduced, stored in or
introduced into a retrieval
system, or transmitted in any
form or by any means
(electronic, mechanical,
photocopying, recording or
otherwise), without
the prior permission of both
the copyright owner and the
publisher of this book.

First published 1997

Typeset by Midland Typesetters
in Baskerville 11/13

Printed and bound by
McPherson's Printing Group
Designed by World of Wonders

National Library of Australia
Cataloguing-in-Publication data:

Sparkes, Graeme, 1951– .

The red island : a journey
around Australia.

ISBN 1 875847 20 0.

1. Sparkes, Graeme, 1951-
– Journeys – Australia.
2. Australia – Description and
travel. I. Title.

919.40463

TO MY MOTHER

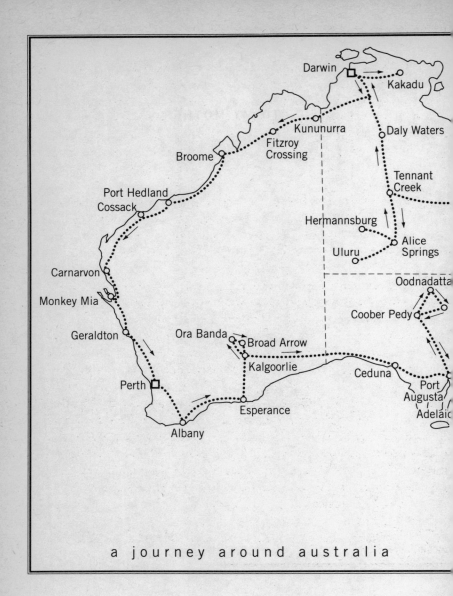

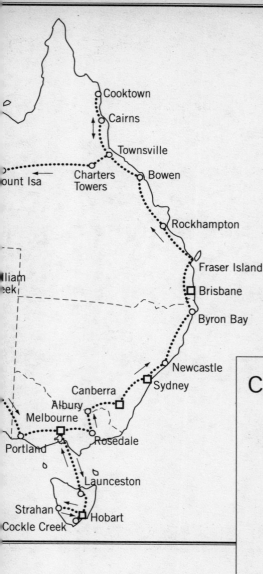

contents

PART ONE
east coast 1

PART TWO
inland 89

PART THREE
lonely road home 141

PART ONE

east coast

LEOPARD TANKS were creeping along Swanston Walk the day I left Melbourne. On any other continent I would have anticipated a change of government. But this was a farewell parade before their redeployment near Darwin, to protect what the armed forces believed was our most vulnerable stretch of coast. It was early July. A feeble sun was doing its best to take the sting out of icy gusts of wind. Dead leaves and paper swirled around the city square. The tanks rolled by. I wondered if I should be grateful; they'd be in Darwin before me. I pulled my beanie down until it covered my ears, zipped my jacket up to the chin and pushed my way through the cheering crowd. A block away, below the steps of Flinders Street Station, a piper in a wheelchair aired a tune for a few cold coins. It was a good day to be leaving.

This trip was twenty-five years overdue. I had planned it with a best friend in my youth; we wanted to travel Australia as soon as we left school. We conspired against our parents, our heads full of adolescent dreams, but somehow our enthusiasm waned as the hour approached. I went off to university, trained as a teacher, and spent several years earnestly pursuing a career.

THE RED ISLAND

Yet travelling was always at the back of my mind. Australia was a land to be traipsed. Its indigenous people were nomadic. Its colonial heroes were wanderers: explorers, prospectors, drovers, shearers, swaggies. This century, truckies, seasonal workers, sales executives and tourists joined the procession. When I was five, Denny, my restless father, became a travelling salesman. With his young family in tow, he roamed the eastern seaboard selling a relatively new Australian invention, the rotary clothes hoist. He must have planted one in every back yard from Wollongong to Brisbane. By the age of seven I'd attended half a dozen different schools. And when we finally settled down in a Victorian country town, I realised that I would never choose to lead a sedentary life.

I started travelling overseas, preferring places with exotic names on other continents, imagining adventure lay elsewhere. I never went around Australia. I never went inland to Uluru, north to Kakadu, west across the great Nullarbor Plain. I never went to Broome, Alice Springs, Mount Isa, Coober Pedy, Kalgoorlie, Oodnadatta—names that rolled around the mouth as magically as Timbuktu.

After I turned forty-three I realised the time had come. I suddenly wanted to make the trip I had postponed for half my life. I wanted to see the entire continent, in a leisurely way and without a schedule in mind, except perhaps to get through the tropics before the Wet set in. I tossed my latest teaching job, packed my old rucksack, bought an all-Australia bus pass. Then at the last minute I decided to leave in style, to start my journey by train, heading east through the picturesque Gippsland region. I intended to go as far as Rosedale, two hundred kilometres from Melbourne: an appropriate first stop, since it was the town where my mother was born.

Beneath the departure clocks at the entrance to Flinders Street Station I pushed past groups of teenagers with

east coast

rampant hormones, bad outbreaks of acne, baggy jeans, huge footwear, and baseball caps placed backwards on their heads. I turned for a final look at the city: the busy intersection, St Paul's Cathedral, Young and Jackson's pub, the old Gas and Fuel building that was earmarked for demolition, the criss-cross of power lines, and, rumbling by now that the tanks had gone, the indefatigable archaic green trams. Four months and fifteen thousand kilometres of travel lay ahead of me.

Tania came from work to farewell me. Standing on the platform, she took photos, gave me a travel clock, and made a few envious remarks about heading north to the sunshine. We had gone overseas together but she didn't want to come on this trip. 'To tell you the truth, I'm glad I'm not going,' she said. 'Some time apart will do us both good.' She managed to sound cheerful. When an ugly diesel engine pulling orange carriages slithered in from Spencer Street Station, I gave Tania a hug and gathered my possessions together. The train stopped long enough for me to board, find a seat, and throw my rucksack onto the rack overhead. The heating was sti-fling. I took off my jacket and beanie, and squeezed past a teenage boy to sit by the window. Then there was motion. And Tania, waving, was soon out of sight. I tried to find some leg room between the sprawling limbs of the passenger facing me. My departure, past the hallowed Melbourne Cricket Ground, over the khaki Yarra River into the suburbs, seemed too low-key to be the start of a journey around the oldest continent in the world.

Travel is a temporary solution. You see it on the faces of travellers, a look of disbelieving relief. They watch the city recede with wild eyes, as if they have pulled off the hoax of the century. The unshaven man in a checked shirt opposite me had the eyes of a scoundrel who'd just duped his own mother out of the savings under her bed. I caught him glancing at the city skyline. He squinted at me fiercely, then disappeared behind his magazine.

THE RED ISLAND

The teenager sitting next to me was a shy blond eighteen-year-old named Nathan, whose burgeoning moustache reminded me of mould spores. The tufts of hair poking out of his baseball cap were greasy, his gangly legs were stretched towards the aisle, and his hands were folded on his belly. He said he was going home to Sale, a town a little further down the track than Rosedale, where he was in his final year at a Catholic secondary college. Next year he hoped to shift to the city himself to study computers. 'That's sensible,' I said, losing interest in him.

I watched the established middle-class suburbs of South Yarra, Toorak, Armadale and Malvern go by. The train stopped briefly at Caulfield then began a slow socio-economic descent to Dandenong.

Now we were racing through the outer suburbs—a vast accumulation of modest brick houses and tidy streets—sweeping through small stations and crossings marked by the urgent clang of bells. At one point I looked through the window and caught sight of a fracture in the uniformity: a towering spout of water from a burst hydrant in an empty street. Nearby, in the middle of the flooded road, was a car on its roof. Not a sign of life anywhere. And then the scene was gone. Trains only stop for crises of their own making. 'Did you see that?' I said.

The man in the checked shirt had seen it, I was sure. But we weren't on talking terms. 'See what?' said Nathan.

As we approached Dandenong station on the outskirts of Melbourne the train seemed to be entering a penitentiary. It ran between two high mesh fences topped with razor wire. Two skinny youths, inmates by the look of them, were amongst the passengers who boarded when we stopped. They sat opposite Nathan who had his cap in his hand and was fiddling with its badge, an emblem of the Houston Rockets. Their heads were shaven except for single peroxided locks that curled in front of their noses.

east coast

Their impassive faces were ghostly, exaggerating the inflammation of pimples. They wore heavy black boots, and one had a surplus army overcoat which he kept on despite the heat. Their proximity made Nathan nervous. He replaced his cap and sat on his hands like a schoolboy in trouble. A woman laden with bags of shopping and a screaming baby sat behind us. The train began to move, and within minutes we were beyond a moribund industrial estate and in the countryside. Green paddocks, cows and low rain clouds. This was the start of Gippsland, a region of Victoria that extended several hundred kilometres to the east coast of Australia.

Immediately I began to relax. I was on my way. I smiled at the shaven-headed youths who reciprocated with studied blankness. I turned to the man who had robbed his mother, prepared for small talk, but he had fallen asleep. I resorted to Nathan. 'Thank God we're finally out of the city.' I rolled my eyes to exaggerate my relief. He sniggered and pressed his chin into his neck. 'What do you think of Melbourne?' I asked.

'It's got better shops than Sale.'

Gippsland was dairy country. Friesians and Jerseys grazed near the tracks. The ground was wet and the tops of hills were under cloud. Dead trees, grey as granite, outnumbered living specimens. Along the fences flowering wattles grew. We passed the towns of Narre Warren and Berwick. I knew this part of Victoria well, but in an hour or so I'd be travelling through relatively unfamiliar territory. I couldn't remember Rosedale where my mother grew up, nor its neighbouring town, Sale, where my grandfather once lived. I asked Nathan what it was like living there.

'Could be worse.' He glanced furtively at the two boys opposite.

'What about work for young people?'

'Esso's just closed down.' The headquarters of Esso-

THE RED ISLAND

BHP's Bass Strait oil fields had been in Sale. 'But there's other work.'

'What sort?'

'McDonald's. Safeway.'

The train ran express from Dandenong to Warragul. It took less than an hour. And when it stopped half its passengers, including the man who'd robbed his mother, alighted. Then the train began to move again. East of Warragul, it passed through a cutting and began to descend into the Latrobe Valley. I caught sight of a power station away to the south as sunlight split the clouds and fell on a long line of chimney stacks.

The Latrobe Valley stank with the pollution from several coal-fired power stations and a paper mill. When I stepped off the train at Moe to stretch my legs, the sulphurous air clung to the membranes in my nose. I took a few strides then clambered back on board. The baby behind me was still wailing. Nathan was blowing his nose. No longer feeling sociable, I closed my eyes and thought about my mother. She had fond memories of growing up in Rosedale on a few acres of land at the edge of town. She had a cow to milk and sheep as pets and siblings who were fond of her. When I told her about my trip, she gave me a list of relatives who had spread around the country, hoping I'd do the right thing and call on them. 'And when you're in Rosedale,' she said, 'don't forget to visit the cemetery.' Two brothers, her mother, her grandparents, and her great-grandfather were buried there.

When I opened my eyes we were passing the Yallourn open-cut coal mine, a hole in the earth large enough to swallow entire towns. If Yallourn itself hadn't been dismantled and relocated, that's precisely what would have happened to it. The power station seemed perilously close to the edge of the cutting. Below, at the bottom of the mine, a machine several times the size of a brachiosaurus grazed on a carbon meadow. 'This whole valley's gonna be dug up

east coast

one day,' Nathan declared, noticing I was impressed.

We stopped in Morwell, where the silent youths from Dandenong departed, and again in Traralgon, the principal town of the region. Then the valley widened to lose its form in undulating pastures. A dead calf near a flooded waterway and more dead trees. Most of the eucalypts that had been spared as shelter for cattle in this green landscape were dead or diseased.

The train had outdistanced the bad weather and entered a pleasant afternoon light. But behind us to the south, over the forested Strzelecki Ranges, storm clouds gathered.

'What sort of work do you do?' Nathan finally asked.

'Recently I've been teaching English to migrants.'

'You don't teach them Asians, do you?'

'As a matter of fact, I do.'

'What do you think of them?'

I knew what motivated a question like that, so I said: 'The Vietnamese I teach are some of the most decent people I've ever met.'

My answer disappointed him. 'Yeah, well, they ought to learn our ways,' he declared. 'Then they'd be all right. My brother lives in Abbotsford. They've taken over down there. All the shops, restaurants, everything. You know what they call Victoria Street these days? Little Saigon! They come here and want to change everything, our religion, our way of doing things, everything we like.'

'But most of the Vietnamese I know are Catholics,' I said. 'Like yourself.'

Rosedale was the next station. It struck me that one of the virtues of travel was the ease with which you could leave people you disliked behind.

After a restrained farewell, I stepped off the train with my rucksack, dressed once more in my jacket and beanie. I stood on the platform alone. The weatherboard station was closed. Despite a neat garden and a recent coat of paint, the

THE RED ISLAND

place looked abandoned. There were padlocks on the doors. The railway shed across the track had been vandalised, with much of its timber torn away. Graffiti covered what remained of its side wall, including a cryptic message: 'Dr Spin—no fear.' I took a quick glance at the weather, slung my rucksack on my shoulders, then went looking for the place where my mother was born.

———

Rosedale, like most Australian towns, had no obvious centre, no plaza or park where the buildings of public importance stood and its citizens could socialise in the evening. Instead, it ranged along the highway, a series of shops and small businesses serving a rural clientele, who drove from their farms and stayed long enough to purchase their supplies, visit their financial consultants, and have a beer at one of the pubs. Several of the shops were empty, adding a touch of desperation to the town's character.

I walked to the Rosedale Motel, a white building with arched windows and a steep Spanish-tiled roof. It looked incomplete. Its owner, Jos de Souza, told me it had originally been designed as a Spanish riding school, but the developer changed his mind and sold what had already been built as a motel. For the next twenty-four years, Jos ran it while his wife, Edith, sold antiques from a large room adjacent to reception.

Jos looked like Albert Einstein: the same walrus moustache, doleful eyes and high forehead. Edith was stout and dressed in black. She appeared briefly to look at their only guest, then returned to her room. I booked in and said, 'This is the site of the house where my mother was born.'

Jos scratched his broad forehead. 'We had two women stay a few years ago who told me they were born here.'

I explained that my mother and her sister had returned

east coast

for a family reunion, and asked him if he knew where the old house had been.

'I showed them, too. Come!' He led me to one side of the motel where a few cypress pines and brambles grew. 'There was a chimney right here that I pulled down,' he said. 'So, this must have been the house.' He waited for my reaction, which apparently disappointed him. 'Right here!' he emphasised. He gestured for me to follow him. 'Under that bush is a well.' He pointed at the spreading bramble. 'When they stood by this well, they cried. Yes, cried! They told me they used to play around here when they were kids.' Still moved by the memory of the sentimental sisters, he shook his head. 'They couldn't believe the changes.' He studied me again for a response. And his scrutiny made me awkward. I would have liked a moment alone. 'Well, nothing stays the same forever,' he sighed. 'Rather a pity, I'd say!'

His refined English seemed at odds with his Portuguese name. As we walked back to the motel I asked him about his origins.

'Yes, you could say I'm Portuguese. But, actually, I'm from Melaka. I learnt English when I was fourteen from Irish Christian Brothers.' His voice had no trace of Irish brogue. 'I was in a Japanese concentration camp with them during the war. When Portugal abandoned its colonies after the war I came to Australia and eventually settled here.'

'It may surprise you,' I said. 'But you aren't the first Portuguese to have lived in Rosedale.'

'No?'

'I suspect my great-great grandmother had that honour.'

'She was Portuguese?'

'So my mother tells me. My great-great grandfather met her near here at Port Albert. Her name was Maria Maxella.' Jos closed one eye and scratched his chin, thinking about the name. 'The problem is, females in genealogies tend to be a sideshow,' I continued. 'I know a lot about her husband, old

THE RED ISLAND

William. Still I believe she beat you here by a hundred years.'

Jos took hold of my arm, led me to the front of the motel, and pointed to a house some distance away on the opposite side of the highway. 'That's where a relative of yours lives. Charlie Robinson. Old chappie. Maybe he'll be able to help you with the family history.'

It was too late to call on Charlie. The rain clouds had delivered a premature dusk. So I walked through the clammy air into town for a meal.

———

It was Charlie who offered to take me to the cemetery to see old William's grave. When I went to his house the next morning, I found him in the back shed seated on a stool amongst rows of stock whips, dog leashes and bridles, plaiting thongs of leather. He had a long crooked nose, high cheek bones, large flat ears and blue watery eyes. He was dressed in shabby brown trousers and a checked coat with a synthetic fur collar. I introduced myself, breathing in the sweet smell of leather while he remembered my mother's immediate family. 'Jim was my cousin,' he said of my grandfather.

'He's been dead for twenty years,' I said.

He rubbed his chin thoughtfully. 'Yeah, you'd be right. I'm getting on myself, you know.' He told me he was seventy-eight, and the last in the family of his generation.

The shed was cluttered with tools and leather. On one wall was an autographed poster of R.M. Williams, the famous supplier of cattlemen's products, clutching a whip that Charlie had made him. 'But I gather you didn't come here to buy one yourself,' he chuckled. 'What do you want to know about the family?'

'What do you know of Maria Maxella, old William Robinson's wife?'

east coast

'Struth, ask me the easy ones!' He pulled himself off the stool and straightened himself slowly. 'I'll tell you what, I'll take you out to the cemetery. See what we can find.'

He took me inside the house to meet his wife, Madge, a plump woman with a gentle smile, who was cleaning a spotless kitchen. She made us a cup of tea and asked me to stay for lunch, but wouldn't sit down and join us.

Driving at walking pace through the streets, he pointed to houses of past relatives: Mick, his grandfather's brother; Bookie Robinson, who ran a tote; the spot in the road where some of his cousins used to milk cows. 'When they got a couple of buckets of cream, they set off to sell it. Money was bloody scarce in those days, boy.'

'You don't have to do this,' I said gratefully, as a light rain began to fall.

He switched on the wipers. 'I don't mind doing nothing as long as it's not in the one place.' A traveller's maxim, I thought. I wound my window down a fraction to smell the wet grass. It evoked the times I lived on farms as a child.

The cemetery was a few kilometres beyond the town, between some open paddocks. A sign warned of redback spiders around the headstones. A few she-oaks stood amongst the graves, and there were pretty finches on the ground. William Robinson's resting place was in a far corner, his headstone so covered with black lichen I had trouble reading its inscription. There was no mention of Maria, no headstone for her.

'I'll show you around the town a bit,' Charlie said.

The farmland ran away towards pine plantations on the ranges. Only once or twice did I set eyes on any cattle or sheep. My grandfather, Jim, used to shear on these properties. Charlie pointed to a farm called Greenacres. 'That was Bob Cornish's place where Jim shore for years.' I could see the old corrugated iron shed where he'd worked, its loose metal sheets ready to flap in the wind.

13

THE RED ISLAND

'And if you see a dance hall within forty miles of Rosedale, Jim would've been there as MC or band leader.' I remembered my grandfather playing accordion or harmonica while my mother patiently tried to teach me the old time dances. 'Jim was a show pony, but a great bloke. And work! He used to do anything. Shearing. Fencing. He used to be the sanitation contractor in the days of shit cans. He was much liked in these parts.'

The rain began to fall heavily. Charlie drove in silence for a while, concentrating on the road, until he pointed to a farm he used to own. 'Eleven hundred acres. I built them old mustering yards from railway sleepers.' He ran a hundred head of dairy cattle. 'Kept us afloat, they did. Paid the bills.' The property ran right to the edge of a pine plantation where kangaroos that had fed on his pastures would shelter. 'The 'roos could ruin you.'

'Did you run anything beside dairy cattle?'

'Sheep, beef, any bloody thing that made money,' he muttered. 'Needed a lot of super to keep the grass good.' He hissed quietly at the memory of his working days. He talked about land prices, and divulged his theory of farming dynasties: the first generation worked hard to build a good business; the second went to college and came home to consolidate the family estate; the third generation also went to college, but turned soft, spent everything, and sold what the two previous generations had spent their lives building. And something else about the latest landed generation annoyed him, too. 'Now they're all buying these exotic cattle. Look at those long-legged buggers.' He pointed to some steers in a roadside paddock. 'They reckon they're shit-hot. But take them to the abattoirs and they're no different from any other breed.'

When we got back to town, Madge had lunch ready for us. I sat at a laminex table while she poured a salty beef stew over toast and made us a cup of tea, reminding me of the meals my mother used to cook.

east coast

Returning to the motel, I saw Jos, who asked me if I'd learnt anything about Maria Maxella. He shrugged at my failure. 'She wasn't the only Portuguese to beat me to this part of the world, you know.' His eyes had a learned glint. 'They were on the south-east coast of Australia, more than two hundred years before Cook came this way. We Portuguese had a valuable spice trade to protect, you see.'

Portuguese traders used to sail to the East Indies around the Cape of Good Hope, a voyage that took two and a half years. And when the Portuguese colonial administrators heard the Spaniard, Magellan, was looking for a shorter route around South America to expedite Spanish trade, they expected him to cross the Pacific at a southern latitude. So they sent their best admiral, Chirlophore Mendonka, down the east coast of Australia to ambush him.

'There's a rock at Green Cape near Two Fold Bay, somewhere south of Eden with "1502" inscribed on it. Mendonka and his crew waited there for four years, but Magellan went up the Peruvian coast and crossed the Pacific closer to the equator, so they missed him. But you could say these Portuguese sailors were the first European settlers in Australia, a long time before the British came.'

I said farewell to Edith who was settled inconspicuously on a tapestry-covered armchair amongst the antiques. As I stepped outside, Jos said, 'Your great-great grandmother probably came from Timor. That was the closest Portuguese colony. Why don't you write to the Catholic Church in Dili? They will almost certainly have records from that time.'

'I might do that one day,' I said. 'But I have a feeling she'll remain a mystery.'

———

I was tempted to take the bus to Eden and search for the rock inscribed '1502'. But on a whim the previous night I

THE RED ISLAND

had rung an old friend who owned a cottage in the hills north of Moe, and pleaded with him to drive me over the mountains to Myrtleford. Twenty years ago we'd worked together there as teachers and later, after we'd both quit teaching, as labourers on tobacco farms.

By nine the next morning we were cruising slowly along the highway towards Sale in his old station wagon. Richard, who usually smoked a joint after breakfast, was blissfully quiet. His face seemed gaunter each time I saw him. He had a square forehead, wide mouth, and narrow jaw. His eyes were soft blue. When we were teaching together we both had long hair and beards; now I was bald and clean-shaven and he was trying to keep up with the times sporting sideburns and a thinning pompadour. His appearance suggested a touch of desperation and mockery. He'd always been a paradox: a self-effacing character who could become exasperatingly stubborn. Ten years ago he'd suffered a stroke that intensified both traits. It also left him with a limp, barely noticeable until he was stoned, a strange marriage of impairment and happiness. I liked his self-deprecatory humour which helped me disregard his fluctuations of mood. But what he thought of me, after twenty years, I still wasn't sure.

When the blues cassette he was listening to ended, he began to comment on the scenery. 'Aren't the wattles lovely in flower.' A little further. 'Lots of cockatoos around here.' Past a river. 'Pelican.' And then, noticing what I'd seen since leaving Melbourne, 'God, so many dead trees!'

We crossed the lower reaches of the Thomson River at Sale, the town where my grandfather had lived for a decade or more. My mother had brought me here once, but nothing looked familiar. The highway went north. Each town we passed was on a river that eventually fed into the Gippsland Lakes, a system of coastal lagoons further to the east. At Bairnsdale we turned off the highway and began the climb

east coast

to Omeo. The road narrowed and the scenery improved.

The towns along the road were small: random clusters of dwellings built together to ward off the sense of isolation that pervades the Gippsland hills. Paint flaked from weatherboards. Junk cluttered yards. And at the edge of each settlement lay a tiny cemetery overgrown with wild grasses. Beyond one town I saw an abandoned timber railway bridge, well above the contours of the land, looking like a rustic aqueduct. And somewhere else, in long wet grass outside a lonely farm house, a small girl wrestled with a wriggling pup.

The heavy station wagon was straining as it climbed. Richard grew sullen. His gaunt features tensed as the road became more tortuous. I watched the scenery and read the signposts. Emu Creek, Eleven Mile Creek—how many Australian creeks had I seen with these names? But there were less common names too. Idly, I began to make lists in a notebook. Of creeks: Ramrod, Monkey, Mullocky, Bullocky, St Patrick's, Barksheds, Lock up, Tuckerbox, Strong, Haunted Stream. Of landmarks: Jews Pinch, Name Stone Point, Dead Horse Flat, Doctor's Flat. Names set my thoughts spinning. Piano Bridge Creek and Price's Downfall. And why the £1000 Bend? The signs were like epitaphs to forgotten history. We travelled through a messmate forest until the land began to roll into a valley.

The road emerged into farmland. Willows and poplars marked the course of the Tambo River. Mistletoe hung from roadside gums. Paddocks where cattle grazed stretched over the hills towards the clouds. I saw a deserted farmhouse stacked with hay in amongst some pine trees, a wedge-tail eagle sailing overhead, a farmer in his home paddock spreading cow pads with a rake.

After Swifts Creek, a timber milling town, the sky began to clear. Richard said, 'Lot of peppercorn trees around here.' We'd been together all morning, but our conversation

17

THE RED ISLAND

hadn't moved beyond the landscape. It occurred to me that in twenty years we'd never discussed anything personal, nothing about our feelings towards each other, and it left me melancholy. We bought sandwiches in Omeo—a town barely touched by modern ways—and ate in silence. Despite the chill in the air the sun had some sting if you stood in the open.

Some way out of Omeo, just as we saw the first snow on the ground, Richard stopped the car to roll a joint. 'Your turn to drive,' he muttered. We swapped places and were soon travelling across level country where the trees were stunted. 'You'll have to drive the rest of the way.' He pressed the cassette button for more music. 'I'm knackered.'

We crossed a snowy meadow. The snow came to the sludgy edge of the road where it banked like a low concrete wall. The sun was pure light in the cloudless sky, making the alpine world warmer than I'd expected. Just before we entered another wood, we saw a sign ordering us to fit snow chains to the vehicle. 'I've got some,' said Richard.

It took half an hour to fit them, but not before we were thoroughly soaked and soiled when I got them tangled around the axle, requiring both of us to squeeze under the car. We removed our sodden jackets and drove off with a length of loose chain, the only piece not properly secured, beating a regular rhythm against a mud guard. Richard rolled himself another number.

By the time we reached the summit of Mount Hotham, he was incapable of speaking. Here the road was burdened with traffic arriving from the Ovens Valley. There were chalets, and carparks full of four-wheel drives. Enthusiasts in garish snow gear strolled beside us, or chatted, or threw snowballs, or laughed into mobile phones. Further off, chair-lifts carried human specks over mighty concave walls of snow. Skiers swept down the brilliant slopes like flies upon a wedding cake.

18

east coast

We began a steep descent with the sun in our eyes. Icicles hung from the snow gums near the summit. I didn't stop until we arrived at the snowline where we removed the chains, had a quick pee that cut little yellow ravines in the last of the white ground, and made a cup of tea with hot water from the thermos. 'The eternal cycle,' Richard muttered.

It took half an hour to get to Harrietville at the base of the mountain. The Ovens River gushed beside the road. Houses hid amongst the vegetation. We followed the river into Bright, an arboreous resort town, popular with second honeymooners. The trees were bare and puddles lay beside the road. Old couples, in coats and scarves and hats, trudged arm in arm along the footpaths.

The highway followed the river. As the sun descended over the end of the Ovens Valley, the steely escarpments of Mount Buffalo to the south lost detail. Colours changed. A soft bronze light filtered through the eucalypts. We skirted the northern contour of the narrow valley floor between rows of bare poplars, past empty fields, where in summer hops and tobacco grew.

Myrtleford was an ugly town at the foot of some steep hills that were being stripped of plantation pines. Despite an attempt to landscape the main street, its commercial character prevailed. It had no civic atmosphere, no sense of community. 'It doesn't change much, does it?' Richard said. 'It's difficult to believe I first came here twenty-five years ago. Almost half my life ago.'

'Looking at you, it's not so difficult,' I said.

'You bastard!' he shouted and grinned.

Richard insisted we drive past the school, which was on the edge of town. It was a long grey building obscured by darkness and bushes that had thickened considerably since our teaching days. Memories flowed: the Volkswagen I came to work in; the briefcase I carried; the pranksters on the staff; a student of mine, a backward country lad, whom the

THE RED ISLAND

principal asked me to counsel after he'd fondled a teacher's breasts; another student throwing a chair at me; the day I taught dressed as the Phantom; Lawrence, my closest colleague, a strange hunched socialist who seemed to have stepped straight out of *The Possessed*. Evidently, Richard's memories were flowing, too. He opened the car door. 'I've waited twenty years to do this,' he said. He walked towards the school and pissed against its gate.

'Let's go to Albury,' I said. 'I've got a friend who'll put us up for the night.'

———

He drove in the dark to Albury, crossed the wide Murray River—its massive redgums obscured by the night—and entered New South Wales. My friend wasn't at home. 'He'll be at the Commercial Club,' I said, getting back into the car.

Paul Wood was a union organiser with the state public service association. He had once led a union delegation to Cuba, and shaken hands with Fidel Castro. Like the legendary communist, he was rotund, bearded and myopic. He suffered a hearing impairment and a propensity to speak in broken Spanish whenever he'd had a few drinks. His social life, it seemed, revolved around the Commercial Club in the main street of Albury, a city that had once been earmarked for development under a failed federal government decentralisation scheme. At the desk I persuaded the receptionist to allow me to look for him in the club bar.

'*Compañero, como estás?*'

'Not bad, Woody,' I said, greeting him with an affectionate hug. I quickly explained my reason for being in Albury. 'Will you put me and my mate up for the night?'

'*Si, si. Pero quieres ... um ... un bebé ... beber, cerveza?*'

'A baby or a beer?'

'Ah ... *una cerveza*.'

east coast

'Later, Woody. We want to clean up first.' He signed us in and gave me the key to his unit.

'*Una cerveza por ti*, mucho later cuando you get back, okay?'

Richard and I went to Woody's unit, showered and returned to the club. Veneer panels and fawn wallpaper had been used to maintain a drab fifties atmosphere. With the crowd of drinkers waiting for the Friday-night lucky-number draw, it took us some time to find Woody, standing unsteadily amongst a group of companions. One of them was Giles, an impish red-headed youth who was loudly informing a sartorial, fresh-faced politician that his chances of becoming prime minister were greatly diminished by consorting with a well-known sympathiser of the Cuba regime. The politician shook my hand with excessive firmness and looked me in the eye. 'Doug Campbell,' he said. 'Currently working with the Australian Workers Union.' Next to him was Dot, a frail old woman holding a glass of stout.

'Hey, *compañeros, comida*?' Woody said. The lucky draw had taken place. He hadn't won. Now he wanted to eat. '*Arriba, arriba.*' He pointed at the ceiling. There was a cafeteria upstairs. Campbell tossed down the remainder of his beer, then left. Giles had already disappeared. Dot followed us upstairs.

The cafeteria was bright and full of diners. Mauve light shades the size of umbrellas hung over the grey tables. The trimmings at the service counters were gilded. As Dot joined us at a table, someone bumped her and she slopped food onto her chair.

Richard wiped the seat clean with paper serviettes and helped her safely into her place. Baubles on her white jumper trembled. She informed us she knew Woody through a mutual interest in Cuba and that she'd lived in North Albury all her life. 'In Union Road,' she added with a degree of satisfaction only an old leftie would feel. 'It used to be farmland.' Her father had owned a small dairy farm, but

THE RED ISLAND

later he subdivided it and built homes for his daughters. There was a well still on her father's land, ninety-five feet deep. 'Dad used to lower mum's jellies down it so they'd set.'

After the meal Woody took us down to the snooker room through several halls of poker machines. Gaudy lights, electronic noises, the periodic metallic spill of coins. Impassive gamblers stared at rolling symbols. Around the walls TV screens displayed the latest Keno lottery results. Woody stopped to look at these momentarily, picked up an entry form, then thought better of it. '*Yo tengo no suerte.*' He was out of luck tonight.

When Woody bent over the pool table as far as his belly permitted, wrinkles appeared on his broad forehead right up to the hairline. He was a competitive player and came from behind to beat me. Then Richard and Dot took over the table. Richard played pool patiently, limping around the table, offering her advice on shots, giving her a second chance when she miscued. It was more of a shared ordeal than a contest—the longest game I'd ever witnessed.

———

Belonging to a nation that occupied an entire landmass obviated certain patriotic tendencies. For one thing, borders were never contentious. We Australians had to look no further than the ocean to recognise the limits of our country, which meant we could afford to be more relaxed about cultural distinctions, traditions, political leaders, national heroes. A certain irreverence prevailed. National heroes were likely to be criminals or shysters. A cultural event could be a mock regatta on a dry riverbed. But it also meant that we could be rather careless with ideals. Our boast of equality was often little more than a demand for conformity, and our involvement in democracy seemed a triennial opportunity to express contempt for our politicians.

east coast

I was on my way by coach to Canberra, the purpose-built national capital, diplomatically located between the country's real centres of power, the old rivals Melbourne and Sydney, and the only major city strategically away from the coast. I wiped the window and tried to watch the scenery: eroded gullies and tracks worn by cattle in the paddocks, dark clouds overhead, sodden earth. 'So what do you think of politicians?' I asked Shane, the youth sitting next to me.

'They suck, don't yer reckon?' he replied.

I shrugged. 'You're not from Canberra?'

'Nah, I'm going skiing up at Perisher.'

The clouds over the mountains to the south of Canberra were the colour of icebergs. 'Looks like you're in luck.'

During winter, Canberra was one of the coldest cities in Australia. People were rugged up in coats and hats. The streets were clean, but nobody stayed outdoors long enough to litter them. I booked into a youth hostel in one of the leafy suburbs, slipped on my gloves and beanie, and went to Civic, the centre of the city, to eat. When I got there around six, it was almost deserted—a few stragglers leaving work, a few young people in rags—a forlorn plaza with a motionless merry-go-round, a fountain statue of a man embracing a boy, and a small brick building that seemed devoted solely to graffiti and posters. Yet I could see its potential. In summer it would be pleasant. Outdoor cafes, no traffic, quiet talk. I walked into a cafe, hoping to meet a local to discuss the merits of summer months in Canberra. Two Pakistani students were telling an Italian how to eat pizza. 'Apply this and you will see how we like it in my country,' said the Pakistani woman, passing a shaker of chilli flakes.

I ate pizza the Pakistani way, and returned to the hostel. I was kept awake that night by the vibrations of a lad—a Christian, judging by the copies of *Everyday Faith* and *Good News for Modern Man* by his side—masturbating in the bunk below me. In the morning, I took a bus back to Civic and

THE RED ISLAND

walked around in icy wind blowing off the mountains. I was the only person that morning to walk across the long bridge over Lake Burley Griffin to the government district. Gusts of rain and spray from a hundred-metre column of water, the Captain Cook Memorial Water Jet rising out of the murky lake, made the crossing unpleasant. Directly ahead, at the end of Commonwealth Avenue and dug into Capital Hill like a warren, was Parliament House. Just off the avenue, next to the monolithic Chinese Embassy, I noticed a dead rabbit being eaten by crows.

Rabbits and the Westminster system: both introduced to Australia by the British. I visited our billion-dollar Parliament House, which had a beautiful foyer, a grand reception hall, and two deserted parliamentary chambers in separate wings rather like musty guests' quarters. There wasn't a politician in sight. They had all fled Canberra for the winter recess.

I spent the rest of the morning inspecting other public buildings, the National Gallery with its fine collection of Aboriginal and early colonial art, and the august High Court where the most far-reaching decree since Governor Phillip set up office at Sydney Cove had been delivered: the Mabo ruling which established in law for the first time that Australia was occupied when the British arrived. Like most Australians, I had heard a lot about Mabo. It had caused consternation in pastoral and mining circles, where the decision was considered an unwarranted obstruction to development. In the cities it had lukewarm support. On this trip I was curious to find out what other Australians thought of it. But for now I took a bus to Civic and, with little to do, copied down the history of the merry-go-round from a nearby plaque.

It was a quaint contraption with German hand-carved wooden horses and twisted upright poles from Scotland, built in 1914 by Herbert Thompson, the engineer who designed Australia's first successful automobile. While I scribbled its

east coast

history into my notebook, someone eating a hamburger approached, and said, 'I don't believe it! Another weirdo with a carousel fetish. What's the fascination?'

'I'm a tourist.'

'Yeah, that's what they all say.' He grinned and bit into the burger. The juice ran down his chin. 'Excellent food! It could do with a few more calories, though.' He wore a woollen coat, a tie, and patent-leather shoes. He had a chubby face and hair tied in a pony tail.

'I'm doing a trip around Australia,' I explained, hoping to foster the conversation. 'So, I felt I ought to visit the national capital. But there aren't any politicians around.'

'Doesn't matter,' he said, wiping the juice off his chin and licking his fingers. 'It's all charades anyway, mate.'

'What is?'

'Politics.' He sidled closer. 'It's a fitting symbol for a political capital, don't you think?'

'The hamburger?'

'I take your point,' he muttered. 'But, no, I was referring to the merry-go-round. Great pity it's not operating.'

'You have to tell me if the kitchen smells,' Beth said. 'I'm so used to it.'

'You've still got mice, then?' The air was stale but I wasn't sure her pet mice were responsible. There were three cages of them beneath a bench. On the kitchen table was an aquarium of fish and an aquarium of frogs. A canary perched in another cage in a corner. All the windows in the house were closed. The blinds were drawn.

Beth lived in the most cluttered semi-detached brick house in Petersham, half an hour from the centre of Sydney. Its verandah was stacked with papers and bottles for recycling, a roll of old linoleum, and scavenged timber for

THE RED ISLAND

firewood. Tied to the branches of a bush overhanging the short path to the gate were a number of two-litre plastic bottles, each containing a couple of centimetres of vile-coloured liquid. 'For trapping flies,' Beth informed me. Her young son Tom elaborated. 'It's urine.' Arrayed along the hallway were two bicycles, more stacks of newspapers, a coat rack burdened with raincoats and sun hats, cartons of cardboard (craft material for school), and bulging cupboards. The bathroom was festooned with washed plastic bags. In the kitchen were various bins for recycling glass, food scraps, plastic and metal. 'Some waste is unavoidable, but I try,' Beth lamented. 'It takes ages to shop. I have to go to forty-four different places if I want to avoid packaging.'

Beth was an energetic, fiercely principled woman with short cropped hair and a pointy nose. She worked as a project officer for Sydney Water, had raised her son alone, and spent most of her spare time campaigning against ecological and social disasters. She asked me how long I planned to stay.

'Just a few days,' I said. 'Long enough to investigate some personal history.'

In the morning she said, 'I'm off to kill a privet up at Tom's school.'

'Good Lord, what's it done? What is it?' I said.

'It's a menace to native vegetation,' she explained, disappearing through the front door with Tom and her gardening tools. 'See you this evening.'

I decided the early memories I wanted to pursue could wait a few days. I caught a bus for the city. An old lady, who boarded a stop later, sat next to me and complained about the weather. She wore an acrylic coat. Her eyes smarted in the cold, and thick cosmetic powder on her face had trapped a tear on her cheek. 'When the wind comes off Kosciusko this time of year, it's freezing,' she muttered.

'Going shopping, are you?'

east coast

'At Newtown. Can't afford the fare to the big complexes, you know. Anyway, I like Newtown. I can watch all the trendies. It's like watching TV. And there's so many nationalities these days.'

'I bet it's changed a lot.'

'Oh yairs.' She said 'yes' in that old-fashioned way. 'Everywhere you look there's someone different. I like guessing where they come from. There's not many of us Aussies left in Newtown, love,' she added. 'Even the ones you think are Aussies turn out to be wogs.'

I got off at Newtown myself, and walked around for a while. It had a grotty charm, a suburb salvaged from ruin by middle-class home buyers who enjoyed the cafe scene and exotic atmosphere that fringe groups and migrants provided. Green groceries, bakeries, newsagencies, book stores, fashion shops and haberdasheries faced the narrow busy street.

In the heart of Sydney, several blocks had been cordoned off because someone was threatening to jump from a building. Emergency services were on the scene. So was a man distributing pamphlets warning that credit cards with micro chips were the sign of the Beast, and that Christ's second coming would occur in a UFO. Then walking along George Street I had a disconcerting experience: a man behind me said hello, and, after I returned the greeting, I realised he was talking on his mobile phone. I fled to the golden top of Centrepoint Tower and looked down upon the city at people reduced to the size of sandflies. From this height the harbour and its famous bridge looked like a broken zipper held together with a clip. The land would slip together if the zipper was ever fixed. Beyond the harbour, the vivid sea and sky merged in a distant haze. I looked across to Manly and decided to take a ferry ride.

At Circular Quay I pushed my way past foreign tourists, commuters, and hard-working buskers. Electric trains clattered along tracks beneath the elevated Cahill Expressway.

THE RED ISLAND

Sydney's buildings seemed to press in upon this area—the landing point of the first British colonists—like a huddle of beasts returning to a cherished waterhole. I recalled Robert Hughes' account of the first fleet's arrival, in *The Fatal Shore*: the voyage to Australia had been so hideous that, upon landing at Sydney Cove, convicts and troopers had fallen into a cathartic nightlong orgy.

It was a relief to get out on the water, beyond the billowy opera house and the bridge's shadow, to view the quay in its entirety. Its western side gave a glimpse into the city's past: warehouses and rows of old tenements, tarted up for tourists and yuppies. I sat outside on a bench against the ferry housing so I could see the harbour, and exchanged a smile with an Indian sitting next to me. He was a graduate in law from Sydney University who had been in Australia for twenty years, the last few in Brisbane because it was more 'laid back' than Sydney. 'Here you're always engaged,' he explained. 'There's no time to stop and think. It's full-on the whole time. How do you know what you're doing is sensible if you have no time to think? It's a party town, too. Work and parties and nothing else. You can't rest here.'

We were distracted momentarily by a woman shouting at a child as he made a valiant attempt to mount the safety rail. The Indian clucked and shook his head. 'Sydney is like Calcutta,' he said. 'A city of eternal movement.' He asked me where I was from. 'Melbourne? Frank Hardy, you know him? He called Melbourne a lady, Sydney a whore, Brisbane an arsehole.'

We were now quite some way from Circular Quay. The shore was lined with apartment blocks. The bridge was out of sight. With a taste of salt in the air, I was thoroughly relaxed and content. As we approached the Heads, the Indian lawyer stopped talking. This was truly a splendid sight. The vertical cliffs left you in no doubt that they marked the entrance to a great harbour, magnificent grey

east coast

walls against which the Pacific Ocean pressed. The sea swelled as we crossed the opening but, even this far from shore, enthusiasts on sailboards swept across the water. Then we were in the shelter of Manly Cove, looking at dozens of apartments built along its rocky edges. The lawyer, who had lived in one of these ten years ago, pointed out what was new. But seeing the ferris wheel near Manly Wharf, he declared, 'Nothing has changed!'

Manly and Bondi, which I visited the next day, were resorts under siege. Whatever appeal their fine surf beaches held was lost to the urban development along the coast. Apartment blocks extended the stratification of cliffs; concrete and bitumen covered the foreshore; stormwater drains disgorged litter into the sea. The pressure of four million people seemed ready to overwhelm the Pacific. While the character of Manly was staunchly middle-class with small concessions to the surfing scene, Bondi was overrun with drifters and budget tourists.

For a day I travelled around Sydney on the suburban trains, getting off at random. Away from the coast it was indistinguishable from other Australian cities, grids of brick and timber houses on modest lots. The promise of hedonism around the harbour faltered in the suburbs. It was hard to find a cheerful face out of sight of the sea. I ventured into the staid northern suburbs and to the outer west, to Penrith and Emu Plains, which had the atmosphere of shanties. From a train window I saw a sign: 'Moving to Mexico. Garage sale.'

One afternoon I went to Kings Cross to look around. At night the suburb, or its few streets of clubs and strip joints, generated a sordid vibrancy that was absent in the daylight hours. It looked washed-out, haggard—beyond lifting its spirits for the night ahead. I saw a pregnant girl lying on a bench near the El Alamein fountain, eating a salami. Then three young prostitutes passed me in a side

THE RED ISLAND

street and sarcastically advised me to smile. 'It seems quiet around here,' I said to an Irish woman who served me coffee in a small cafe.

She agreed and blamed the current inquiry into police corruption. 'Everyone's ducking for cover.' There were no other customers, so she slid into the seat opposite me. 'I don't know what all the fuss is about. They ought to leave them alone or pay them a decent wage. It's the same the world over. Who'd want their job? Look at those two buggers that got shot dead up north the other day. Two cops. The big brute shot them through the head. Don't tell me he wasn't trying to kill them.'

'We could still do with a few honest cops, don't you think?'

'Everyone's corrupt. Police, businessmen, politicians. Look at how those politicians get all those gifts and things. What's that if it's not corruption?'

'What about the violence around here?' I asked. 'You hear a bit about that on the telly.'

'There's not much, really. I think there's more violence elsewhere, like Redfern.'

'Why Redfern?'

'That's where the Aboriginals live. They'll bash you in the street.'

'Any street in particular?'

'Eveleigh.'

Redfern had the largest concentration of urban Aboriginals in Australia. It was the centre of much of the political agitation for land rights and improved welfare for indigenous people. It had a history of confrontation between residents and police, and the Eveleigh Street district had a reputation as Australia's worst urban slum. Since arriving in Sydney, I'd twice heard you couldn't walk its length without being attacked by Aboriginal residents.

I decided to visit Eveleigh Street. I skirted the neighbour-

east coast

hood and entered the street from the direction of the train station. If someone confronted me about my intrusion I could say I was rushing to catch a train. But soon I felt foolish about the precaution. Most of the houses were double-storey brick tenements. Some were gutted or boarded up, others were in terrible disrepair, but many seemed well tended despite the wear of poverty. Doors were open, children played around old cars in the street, residents were on the footpaths chatting in small groups. Nearer the station there was an enclosed garden and adventure playground. No-one took much notice of me, but I rather envied the sense of community I had glimpsed. If I had ever experienced that in any neighbourhood where I had lived, it hadn't been since childhood.

At the end of my daily excursions I played soccer with Tom. After dinner Beth made sure my education was on track. She talked about environmental degradation. She took me to *Politics in the Pub* at the Charlie Park Hotel. And another time we went to a huge rally at the Town Hall to protest the French resumption of nuclear testing in the Pacific. Finally, I turned my attention to my own history project.

My father's brief career as a travelling salesman began in Sydney, after years of discontent in other jobs. Denny had left school when he was twelve and undertook an apprenticeship in carpentry, but at the end of World War II he was conscripted into the occupational forces. When he returned from Nagasaki, he couldn't settle into the construction trade. He married and worked for his father, a plasterer, for a couple of years, then suddenly left his home in Launceston, lived with his young family for a while on Flinders Island in Bass Strait, shifted to Victoria, then back to Tasmania. Denny was a handsome man, with wavy hair and restless blue eyes. He was muscular from his training as a boxer in the army, and had boundless energy, which he didn't seem

THE RED ISLAND

to know how to harness. In the fifties, when Australia had recovered sufficiently from two decades of austerity, its citizens began to consider making their lives more comfortable. New inventions to help around the house were on the market: pop-up toasters, washing machines, motor mowers, rotary clothes hoists. People had money to spend. My father's disposition and Australian society were heading for an historic encounter.

I was determined to find, if not the house where we'd lived temporarily while he was selling clothes hoists around the suburbs, at least the school I'd attended. I borrowed Beth's street directory and took a train south as far as Hurstville, then caught a bus to the other side of Botany Bay to Sylvania Heights. There, at the edge of a neighbourhood of vinyl-cladding houses, I found the primary school surrounded by pine trees, still with a temporary prefabricated look about it. I hadn't anticipated the pleasant effect this would have on me. I had spent much of my young life changing homes, schools, towns, states. My past was spread over half the country, impossible to trace comprehensively. All I had left were fragments of memory. To trace the source of one of these phantoms gave me a good deal of satisfaction.

Across the road from the school I noticed some people on a landing at the rear of a house. Looking over the side fence I spied an old rotary clothes line in the yard. On impulse I made my way down a path at the side of the house and, without introducing myself, came straight to the point. 'Excuse me. This may sound like an odd question, but how long have you had your Hills Hoist?' When the elderly couple gaped in alarm at me, I gave them a reassuring smile.

'About forty years,' the old boy mumbled.

'I thought so! My father used to sell them around here.' I gestured towards the clothes line, a sturdy cast-iron pole supporting a pyramidal frame of wires and lesser poles exactly in the centre of a lawn, dominating the back yard,

east coast

like a sculpture. A narrow concrete path led from the back steps to the line. 'I was thinking that might be one of his. Still in good nick, is it?'

The elderly woman, less alarmed than her husband, nodded and sighed. 'Oh, yeah, she's been a beauty.'

'I've seen a few modern ones around,' I said. 'But they look pretty flimsy. Not like that. What's it been like living here in Sylvania Heights?'

'Lovely, just lovely,' she said.

'Never travelled?'

'Not really,' she said. 'We've been up to Surfers a couple of times.'

'Well, thanks for talking to me.'

I strolled around Sylvania Heights trying to spot old Hills Hoists, which I was prepared to believe my father had sold—his contribution to Australian culture.

Denny never relaxed enough to walk anywhere. With one hand in a pocket to prevent his small change rattling, he jogged from place to place, even if it was just down the street to buy cigarettes. He had the perfect temperament for a travelling salesman. And he told me before he died (finding contentment in his last few years selling cheap earrings at flea markets around Victoria), it was the one thing he was good at. The rotary clothes line was an easy sell. He moved around suburbs on foot, peering into backyards until he saw a woman hanging out washing along loose untidy lines.

After several profitable months around Sydney, he had moved us further north, first to a house on the shore of Lake Macquarie, near Newcastle, then on to Brisbane. With the successful return to Sylvania Heights behind me, I thanked Beth and Tom for their hospitality and set out to retrace the rest of our footsteps.

THE RED ISLAND

It took an hour to get through Sydney onto the express-way north, which ran through rocky scrubland, across the wide Hawkesbury River and into hilly country where bushfires had charred the earth. The smelly, guitar-wielding traveller next to me fidgeted and ate jelly beans. I dozed in preference to a conversation about favourite colours, and woke when the driver's mobile phone rang as we descended to the coastal plain.

I liked Newcastle the moment I saw its old buildings and wild beaches. I liked its grimy port and steelworks, the labyrinth of metal conduits, the massive buildings, the fuming effluent, the cranes, the ships. I walked along a breakwater, built almost two centuries ago by convicts at the mouth of the Hunter River, to a lighthouse on a bluff known as Nobbys Head; I climbed to Fort Scratchley which afforded a great view of the port and the steel works; I fol-lowed the shore to an old swimming pool hewn into a rock shelf, again by convicts, where the Dixon Park 'coldies' winter swimming club met on Sundays at 10 a.m. The city had a charm capable of withstanding environmental criti-cism. I went looking for a local to chat with.

At a cafe on Hunter Street, I fell into conversation with Carlos, a thick-set, middle-aged Spaniard, who had lived in Australia for nearly forty years.

'Why did you come to Australia?'

'A mistake,' he said, and burst into laughter, as if it were the most plausible of reasons. He had kindly eyes which almost closed when he grinned. He threw up his hands and added, 'A girl. She fell in love with somebody else. I wanted to get as far away from her as possible.'

'What happened to her?' I asked.

'She got married.'

'And you?'

He shrugged and sipped his drink. '*Soy siendo mozo*. Still single.'

east coast

'But you must like Australia to have stayed.'

'If you're asking me, in the last ten years it's gone down-hill. Murders, robberies, assault, that's all you hear about these days. No work, either. I haven't had a job for eight years.'

When he first came to Australia, it wasn't such a bad place. He had migrated as an indentured labourer on the Snowy Mountains Scheme, where he worked for a couple of years. After he left, it was easy to get work. He'd cut sugar cane near Mareeba on the Atherton Tableland in Queensland. Then he worked on oil rigs in Bass Strait for a decade. 'Now for eight years I'm unemployed. But I'm not on the dole.'

I noticed he wore a gold ring with an embedded dia-mond that alone would have rendered him ineligible for social security.

'I own a hotel in Granada,' he said. He had returned to Spain seven or eight times. 'But Granada is too expensive to live. Why should I go back there?' He sounded defensive. 'I have some businesses here in Newcastle, too. This cafe is mine, for example.' He waved his arm around. 'Anyway, I've spent as much of my life in Australia as Spain. Which is my home?'

One morning I caught a bus to the suburb of Belmont and walked a few blocks to Lake Macquarie, a broad expanse of water as salty as the sea. A cold wind swept across it, causing a flotilla of moored yachts to rock like metronomes. Stinking seaweed cluttered the thin strip of beach. I walked along the shore scrutinising the double-storey houses. None resembled the image I had in my head. I sheltered from the wind behind a sailing club and tried to remember my stay here, but could only conjure up pelicans on the lake and the *Mickey Mouse Show* on TV.

Disappointed, I returned to Newcastle. The recreation room at the backpackers' hostel was crowded with drifters watching TV and playing pool. Some of them were old,

THE RED ISLAND

with faded tattoos and wrecked faces; others were wild-looking teenagers. A few of them were picked up for work each morning at dawn and taken to building sites. I tried to have a conversation with a boy whose small head was wrapped in a torn bandanna. 'How's things?'

'Well, I'm still alive.'

'Bad day, huh?'

He told me he'd just lost his job and didn't know why. I advised him to speak to his union.

'I'm not in one,' he said. 'They just bleed money out of you, man.'

'They might've been able to help you.'

'If I was in a union, I wouldn't have got the fucking job in the first place.' He walked away.

I wanted to update my journal, so I found a pub a few blocks away that was almost empty and wrote steadily for an hour.

'I don't mean to be rude,' I heard a woman say. 'But what are you writing?'

'When I travel I keep a journal,' I said.

She stepped alongside me, an attractive plump woman in her early fifties who had been drinking with three men still seated at the bar. 'Mind if I sit down?' Her head lolled as she dragged the chair back. One of her eyes was black and swollen. 'You going to write a book or what?' As she lit a cigarette, I noticed she wore two diamond-studded rings.

'Maybe. What's your name? I can put it in it.'

She squinted at me and licked her bottom lip circumspectly. 'Guess.'

'I can't. There are too many names.'

'Guess,' she insisted.

'Joan.'

'That's so common,' she muttered in disgust.

'Sorry. You'll have to tell me.'

She frowned. 'You know, I honestly can't remember what

east coast

it is.' She carefully articulated each word. 'I like to see a man writing. Why are you bald?'

'I'm middle-aged.'

'No you're not. You shave it!'

'It looks better that way.'

'A bald man writing,' she mused. She reached over and took the pen from me. 'You know, my husband's over there. I don't do this too often.'

While I glanced anxiously at the group of men, she wrote a phone number on my notebook. 'Are you sure you can't remember your name?' I asked stupidly. She got up and, as she walked away, ran her hand across my shoulder.

The next morning I went for a walk to the sea, watched small rainbows in the spray, then found a phone box. Giving the woman's phone number a wistful glance, I rang the bus company.

———

The coach went north along the coastal highway, but most of the way the ocean was out of sight. Sturdier, greener eucalypts grew in the forests. The sun was getting stronger, flickering through the foliage like a strobe light. Most of the passengers were young foreign tourists on their way to Queensland. They were watching a video, *Jurassic Park*, on a small screen above the driver's head, while just outside their windows was lush primeval forest.

After Port Macquarie, a town enjoying a population boom with new housing estates and shopping complexes— where the sea, catching the afternoon sun and a swirling wind, looked like boiling mercury—an English tourist sat next to me and shouted, 'I say, you're not a VIP, are you?' I thought he was sneering at me, but it was the smile of some- one whose upper lip was missing. He adjusted his glasses and squinted.

THE RED ISLAND

'Not yet,' I said. 'Would I be travelling on buses if I were?'

This time he did sneer—with incomprehension. He turned away and tapped the girl in front of him on the shoulder. 'Excuse me. Excuse me. Where are you staying in Byron Bay? You see, I've booked into one of the backpackers' hostels and I wasn't sure if it was the cheapest?' After they discussed accommodation and she'd told him where she was staying, he said, 'Do you get a VIP discount there?'

The Backpackers' Association discount. I tapped him on the shoulder. 'I'm YHA,' I said.

When the girl told him her booking was cheaper, he slumped into his seat and groaned. He looked miserable. He fidgeted with a plastic bag beneath his seat, pulled out a loaf of white bread and began to eat a slice.

The afternoon light had relinquished its harshness. Mauve and amber filtered through the eucalypt haze, softening the ranges. We stopped in Coffs Harbour to let some geriatrics alight. This was the start of the retirement belt, a stretch of coast colonised by Australians who had lived through World War II, worked all their lives in cities, and were determined to see out their days in a balmy climate.

Another movie started and the Englishman sighed. He pulled out another slice of bread, took a bite and chewed until there was a ball of grey dough in his mouth. Out the window I saw a banana plantation.

It was dark when we arrived in Byron Bay. The coach was met by a troop of smiling touts holding placards that promoted hostels. I had been in Byron Bay eighteen years before. The town had metamorphosed from a quiet seaside village that hippies had recently discovered to a bustling holiday resort. The touts represented the low but most lucrative end of the market; at the other end, controversial plans for an eighty-five million dollar Club Med resort were before the local council committee.

east coast

Next morning I walked along the beach to the cape, the most easterly point on the Australian mainland. Dolphins frolicked just offshore. During the hottest part of the afternoon, I returned to town and found a pub that had yet to sanitise its ambience to please tourists. Customers drank beneath television screens that transmitted horse races, placing bets with the TAB at the bar. Most of them were men with tight navy shorts and singlets stretched over their bellies. But the fellow I sat beside wore a blue cotton hat, a Hawaiian shirt and a dirty cardigan. 'I'm Les,' he said. 'Just minding me own business and having a quiet bet on the gee-gees.'

'Mind if I join you, Les?'

'Why not? You've done nothing against me that I know of,' he said, frowning. His glasses, which had lost their lugs, lay on his form guide. 'Are you a betting man, yourself?'

'Not me. My old man was, though,' I said. 'He was a bloody demon for the horses.'

Les shook his head in sympathy. 'Look under me stool,' he said. I looked and saw two crinkled plastic bags. 'All I've got left on this earth. The gee-gees and the grog, mate, they can ruin yer. Ruined me.' He began to laugh but wheezed, coughed and went red. He reached for his fags. 'Jesus!'

When he managed to control his breathing, I said, 'You must've worked once.'

'I used to be in the navy years ago. My commander got himself discharged because of the drink, an alcoholic, like meself. After I got out, I moved here and there, you know, Newcastle, Ballina, Brisbane, back to Sydney. A hundred smackeroos in me pocket, that's enough to get by. You carry any more than that and it can get yer into trouble in more ways than yer can count. I'll tell yer something, I got an aunty who's filthy rich. She's got a house as big as this pub up in Toowoomba. A mate of mine asked me what I was going to do with all her dough when she dies, and I told him

THE RED ISLAND

I hope I kick the bucket first. That's the truth.' He wheezed and pointed at his cigarettes and beer. 'Money can be a killer.'

'If you can't manage it,' I said.

'Know your capabilities, that's my philosophy. The grog's a killer. I've had four girlfriends die on me. Drinking partners. Not, you know, shagging partners. When you're on the demon drink you're not interested in that. They liked the drink and the horses, come down the pub and have a few bets.'

'You live here?'

'No, mate, not any more. I'll stay here a few days. See how it's going, like. I'll probably head back to Ballina. They know me at the bank there. The bank manager wants to know what I want the money for. When I tell him, he says I'm a bullshit artist and I just want it for booze and cigarettes, so I says to him, "You look a bit under the weather yerself." And I get me dough. Nice place, Byron, eh? You can doss on the beach easy enough. Anyway, it's usually the cops who decide when I move on.'

'How do you find dossing on the beach? Must be a bit hard on you?'

'I'm sixty percent physically of what I should be. But mentally and spiritually I'm one hundred percent. No bullshit, mate. I'm at peace with meself.'

On the second day I visited Nimbin, a town in the mountainous hinterland that had hosted the seminal Aquarius festival a quarter of a century ago while I was still at university. I remember the enthusiasm of students who were going to revolutionise society with tolerance and peace and communal living and music and marijuana and alternative medicine. Ignoring the hostility of locals who felt their farming community had been invaded, the students painted rainbows on shop walls and bought shares in communes, changing Nimbin, but little else, forever.

east coast

Inside the small folk museum in the multicoloured main street, I read: 'In Nimbin now there's a real sense of a new community, a tribe of people who actually love and support each other ... It's spiritual.' Outside a sullen group sat near the museum entrance, united in its unwashed dishevelment and a hatred of the enemy, two detectives, who were searching a car a hundred metres further down the street. I asked a toothless, tattooed hippie about the cops. 'Once or twice a week they come here, man,' he said. 'Drug busts.'

'They still hassle people about dope around here?' I said, surprised.

'It's heroin these days, man.'

In the evening when I returned to Byron Bay the youth hostel was having a cheap barbecue—all the meat and alcohol you could consume for seven dollars. I sat next to a Tasmanian couple who were returning from a honeymoon on the Gold Coast, where they had been overwhelmed by the number of Asian tourists. 'They didn't beat us with guns, but they've beaten us with big bucks.'

'Don't Nick. That's enough,' the girl sniggered.

'I'm just starting,' Nick warned, holding his glass of Moselle aloft. 'Give me a few more of these and I'll be on my way. Crikey, I bloody hope there's no Asians sitting here.'

His wife giggled. 'Oh, don't Nick, please. I know some nice Asian girls.'

In the morning I got up before dawn and climbed to the lighthouse on Cape Byron to watch the first rays of the sun strike Australia. Then I caught the bus to Coolangatta on the Queensland border. Before I retraced the final part of my father's trail in Brisbane, I wanted to visit an old friend.

'You'll fit in okay,' the Colonel reassured me, his huge hand ushering me into the cafeteria at Coolangatta's Twin

THE RED ISLAND

Towers Services Club. 'They're either bald or old in here.' At eighty-two he felt he could joke about the elderly. He chuckled deeply, stretching his neat moustache to the creases in his cheeks.

I stepped into a deep hall filled with grey heads. 'You're right. It's like a waiting room at the necropolis.'

'Eh, what did you say?' He gave his hearing aid a few forceful taps. 'This dashed thing never works in public.'

The Colonel was the father of a friend of mine, a retired army officer, who had followed half the superannuated population of the southern cities to the Gold Coast. I had known him since I was a teenager. Whenever he returned to Melbourne we played a round of golf. Despite his age he invariably urged me to play an extra nine holes.

After the meal, he and his wife, Yasuko, showed me around the club, the restaurant, the auditorium and the gallery of the stars who'd performed there, the rooms of poker machines and Keno screens. Then the Colonel drove us to their villa at Banora Point, cutting across lanes and the paths of other cars at roundabouts, frustrating other traffic by travelling slowly in the fast lane, braking erratically, making me more nervous on the road than I had been since leaving Melbourne.

In Tweed Heads, the New South Wales city adjoining Coolangatta, some elegant elevated timber houses with carved art-nouveau panels in the parapets still existed. But across the Tweed River at Banora Point every residence I saw was modern brick. Most of the estate had burgeoned in the past two years, including a shopping centre and Club Banora.

While we walked around the shopping centre, I asked him why he preferred Banora Point to Melbourne. 'It's friendlier here,' he said. 'Look at this woman coming. She'll probably give us a smile.' As she approached, his own broad grin almost dislodged his dentures. The woman would have

east coast

needed the emotions of a fish not to reciprocate. 'What did I tell you?' he whispered.

The Colonel still had the poise of an army officer. Despite his age he walked erect, almost marched, even in his villa unit. He was gruff, autocratic, decent. It seemed quite remarkable that thirty-odd years in the army hadn't changed his conviction that most of Australia's social problems could be solved if only the powerful were less greedy. One evening, while we were watching the TV news, he said, 'When it comes to the crunch, my boy, those blighters think only of themselves, not the poor worker in this country.' He was at odds, too, with the leaders of the Returned Services League on the issue of republicanism. 'They're scared they'll lose their Queen's honours.' Knowing he had been awarded an MBE, I smiled. 'But the crux of it is, we'll never be a real bloody nation until we're a republic. What have the Brits done for this country except steal it in the first place?'

There was little he enjoyed more than an earnest political argument. Appreciating his company, I stayed up with him in the evenings to debate world affairs. I felt sorry for him that politics were of no interest to Yasuko. She had been in Australia since the end of World War II, but if the topic was politics her English deserted her entirely. Her flat cheeks would blossom in a grin and she would walk away. When I asked her if she would ever contemplate living in Japan again, she said, 'Oh no, no. Australia much nicer, much more cheaper. Hospitals more expensive in Japan.'

But she hadn't abandoned her native land entirely. The unit was full of Japanese trinkets and decor. A large urn stood near the entrance. Flower arrangements and wooden dolls adorned small tables. And several sumi paintings hung on the walls. In the living room was a small Buddhist shrine where Yasuko said a prayer before dinner.

At dinner, the Colonel talked about war. 'It's a terrible thing,' he said. 'And those who glorify it are bloody fools.' He

THE RED ISLAND

had never been to an Anzac Day ceremony since his retirement, but now that he was getting older he liked to reminisce about his army days. One afternoon, while waiting for Yasuko to complete her exercise class at a Qigong centre somewhere in the hinterland of the Gold Coast, I walked with him along a rainforest track, listening to stories about his experiences in New Guinea. 'We used to have to hack our way through jungle like this here with machetes.' He had contracted malaria and dengue, and was involved in the Battle of Shaggy Ridge, one of the last battles of the war in New Guinea. He was given the air traffic controller's job at Pundu in Ramu Valley. 'Holy powers of piss, it was only a hundred and fifty yards wide. One day a Zero strafed us.' There were three of them and they dived into a trench. 'It came that close I could see the Jap's face, poor blighter.'

At the end of Yasuko's session at the Qigong centre, the Colonel and I were invited into the massage room while an instructor showed her some three-circle exercises. 'You've got to cut the suit to fit the purpose,' the Colonel said when we were asked to join in. 'I play bowls for my exercise.' The ceiling, floor and walls of the room were pine. A full-length mirror allowed clients to observe and correct their techniques. The Colonel whispered, 'When she first started coming here, she never used to fart. Couldn't. Had to take tablets for wind. But on her first day here she bloody near blew the wall down.'

He drove us along the Gold Coast, through the urban canyon of Surfers Paradise, around new secured estates like Robina, where mansions lined artificial waterways. I asked the Colonel to drop me in Surfers so I could look around more thoroughly. He arranged to pick me up later in Coolangatta.

The beach that had fostered Australia's most popular holiday resort was in shadow, a sublime stretch of coastline that had been transformed into something quite ordinary by

east coast

zealous high-rise development. Holiday makers in bathers sat shivering stubbornly, gazing at the choppy sea. Crowds promenaded, hordes of people in loose summer wear, with ice creams or soft drinks in their hands, and looks of contentment on their faces. I saw a young teenage girl in a t-shirt with *Juicy* printed across her chest. In a food mall I sat next to an astronomy student from Canberra who was in Surfers for the adventure parks: Movie World, Sea World, Wet'n'Wild. 'Fantastic rides at Wet'n'Wild,' he said. 'You're stomach's in your mouth. Your brain is rattling.' I asked him what part of astronomy he was studying. 'Cosmology. The big picture.' Next he was going to Ripley's Believe It or Not! 'Sounds like fun,' he said. The big picture. Brain-rattling rides. His mind was moving faster than the speed of light.

In a pub, where I went for a beer, a buxom girl in mustard shorts flirted long distance with some beefy tattooed men around a pool table at the far end of the bar, while her girlfriend asked her why she bothered. 'It's all that brawn,' she explained.

I suddenly missed my friends. Although I was fond of the Colonel, I wanted to talk to someone who would appreciate how I was feeling. So I decided to ring Tania. She was missing me too, and wanted me to return by Christmas. While we made some tentative plans, I noticed a barefoot adolescent wrapped in a threadbare blanket, who had stopped at a rubbish bin nearby to search for scraps. I watched him retrieve a half-eaten hot dog. I hadn't expected this in Surfers Paradise. I said goodbye to Tania as the derelict headed for another bin.

'Do you want a proper meal?' I called to him.

He looked at me impassively. 'Yes, mate,' he replied.

'Your choice,' I said. We went off to McDonald's.

THE RED ISLAND

Brisbane was a wall of glass around a bend in the wide Brisbane River. It exuded optimism, brashness and confidence. Within a hundred years, it was expected to be Australia's pre-eminent city. My nephew Joel had transferred here after his employer, a Melbourne computer firm, expanded its operations. 'This is where they expect the market to develop,' he said.

Joel was taller than me and a good deal more robust—a physique he had inherited from his Polynesian father. It still astonished me how someone I once cradled in my arms had outgrown me. He shook my hand and welcomed me into the villa he rented in the southern Brisbane suburb of Daisy Hill. His face and the knuckles on his hands were bruised from a melee in a recent rugby match. 'I got into my first ever football brawl,' he explained, shaking his head. 'I don't believe in fighting on the ground. But one of their players attacked my mate, who was already groggy from a heavy tackle.' His swollen hands lifted one of his infant daughters into the air. Wide-eyed delight stole her breath and momentarily displaced her curiosity in the stranger talking to her father. He turned to his wife. 'It's true, Nizanne, isn't it?' he said, 'about me not getting into fights.'

Nizanne shrugged, a faint smile on her face. 'It's true,' she conceded. But there was nothing servile in her tone. She was a confident young woman with proud eyes and a firm jaw. 'Joel's got a temper sometimes, but he can control it.'

They invited me to stay. It was a new double-storey unit with wood chips covering the small back yard to prevent the spread of weeds. Inside the rooms smelt unused; the paint seemed barely dry. I sat in a modern leather lounge suite while Nizanne brought me a coffee. 'I've got enough money now to take my kids to Samoa this Christmas,' Joel told me. 'They've never been. My family over there haven't seen them yet.'

I felt a pang of envy—family to stay with on a South Pacific island! When Joel was a teenager—with his mother's

east coast

encouragement—he had made contact with his relatives in Western Samoa and spent a year at school in Apia. By the time he returned to Australia, he had lived communally with his clan, learnt to speak Samoan and discovered he had a place in Samoan society if he ever chose to return permanently.

After Joel put his daughters to bed, I told him about wanting to find the house where I had lived when I was not much older than his daughters, during my father's final episode as a travelling salesman. My mother had given me the name of the street and the suburb, although not a house number. We looked in a street directory, and the following day he took me into the city, where I caught a bus to Kelvin Grove.

There were certain things I remembered well about the year we spent in Brisbane. From the day we arrived we lived under an alias, or more accurately, two aliases. I'm not sure why, but I like to think it was a precaution rather than something more devious. But remembering which surname applied to which occasion was a considerable challenge for three children under the age of seven, and quite a dilemma, too, since we had a mother who daily impressed upon us the importance of honesty. I remembered the house had a brick fence but was built of weatherboards on a slope with a room underneath at the back, and a garage at the bottom of a steep driveway. I remembered a huntsman spider in the garage that we liked to let crawl over our arms, a banana plant outside and a view across a valley to a lush range of hills. I remembered the adjacent house where every day a man used to yodel in the bath. I remembered the walk to school, and skipping barefoot in the gutters on rainy summer afternoons. I remembered a stranger who tried to entice me into her car and how I ran home in panic. An odd mixture of fond and anxious memories. It is curious, too, how early in life we start to develop certain traits. I had learnt discretion by then. When my elder sister tried to get

THE RED ISLAND

me to kiss the neighbour's daughter in the space underneath our house, I kept it secret from her that I'd already performed far more daring acts with the girl as she sat on our front fence post and her father yodelled in the bath.

I recognised the fence post immediately, and the slope down to the garage. There was even a banana plant growing in the yard. I skulked up and down the street, looking at the place from different angles. I walked to the school, a dour double-storey brick building, and more memories besieged me: free lunches in the canteen each day; an old man offering sweets to children in the bushes near the back fence; children playing cricket and flying paper aeroplanes; a flawless recital of my reader and an incursion into a higher class to perform for my proud teacher only to find I couldn't read a word of a different book; a classmate asking me why I had two last names.

My father must have done well with his sales of clothes hoists because we stayed almost a year, and I have scant memory of him taking time to do anything with his children. There were long periods when he was away. Perhaps he had gone further north, seeking new markets, without the burden of a young family.

Four decades later, the rotary clothes hoists were still in back yards all the way up the Queensland coast to Cairns and beyond, where I was now headed.

From Brisbane I travelled on a coach past the glistening conical peaks of the Glass House Mountains and through the suburban sprawl of the Sunshine Coast. Noosa Heads was at its northern tip, a tourist resort, whose commercial centre was in the same architectural style I'd been seeing all the way along the east coast: metal tubing and grids featured around courtyards and walkways. Aqua, pink and

east coast

grey predominated. Elegant palms provided an exotic tropical illusion. I booked into a hostel, then headed for Alexandria Bay. A walk through the scrub around the rocky coast was just the tonic I needed.

When I reached the bay, I traipsed across sand to the sea which surged and sucked on a steep beach. When I was here on a holiday almost twenty years earlier, hippies used to live in tents and humpies at the southern end of the bay. I had camped with them. It had been almost obligatory to go about naked, and I had swum in the sea in the nude for the first time since my second birthday. Now there was no camping and no hippies, although there were still nude bathers, young men with stylish haircuts and supple bodies who pranced through the breakers or lay on towels between small sandy rises. I kept walking, past the outlet of a creek whose water—after the hippies had assured me it was safe to drink—had blessed me with orange diarrhoea. At the far end of the beach, the wooded land came down to the sea, an ancient flow of lava that had set like fudge against the water. I spent the afternoon sitting alone on the low black cliffs watching the swell of the sea.

The town of Hervey Bay was on a flat piece of coast, a few hours north of Noosa. Without the recent upsurge of interest in whales and the placement of the Fraser Island National Park on the World Heritage List, it might have remained an obscure holiday village for anglers. An aggressive push into the top end of the tourist market was changing its character. Luxury accommodation sat awkwardly beside old fibro-cement cottages. A smelly grey beach that only pelicans used was kept from sight by thick vegetation along the foreshore. A modern shopping complex had recently opened in anticipation of a large population growth.

THE RED ISLAND

I decided to see Fraser Island. I stayed overnight in a busy backpackers' hostel, and put my name down for an organised four-wheel drive tour of the island. When I went to a briefing with sixty others, I was assigned to a group of friendly British tourists. While we were organising supplies for three days, one of them said, 'What grog are we taking? That's the main thing.' There were nine of us. Half went to the supermarket; the rest found a bottle shop.

Back at the hostel, the bar was full of revelling young tourists. There was hardly a person in the room over thirty. When I went to my dormitory to pack enough clothes for three days I thought the room was empty and began to sing. But soon I felt a presence. The bunks were arrayed around the walls and the one next to mine had a towel hanging from a cross beam, blocking my view of its lower mattress. I looked behind the towel and found myself inches from a couple who were silently fucking.

I jumped back mumbling apologies. They giggled and praised my singing. I returned to the bar and had a brandy. I'll give them an hour, I thought. I went for a walk along the beach road as far as Vic Hislop's Shark Show. It was shut, but I gratefully inhaled the powerful seaweed stink of the bay. When I returned the couple were still at it. I muttered a remark about the stamina of the young, and left. The bar was getting rowdier. A girl stood on a chair, ready to remove her bikini top. I watched her until someone popped up in front of me—the lipless Englishman I had travelled with in northern New South Wales. 'Well, well, well. Fancy meeting you here!' he said grinning, as if he had found a long lost friend. 'I suppose you're here for Fraser Island and the whales.'

It was early August, the start of the whale-watching season. 'Not the whales I'm afraid.'

'Me neither. Too expensive.'

To escape him I returned to the dormitory. I went

east coast

straight to the lovers' bunk and whipped the towel away. 'Time's up!' I said. The bunk was empty.

In the morning, hungover backpackers prepared for the trip. As we checked the camping gear, a hire company delivered six four-wheel drive vehicles. Our group was the first to leave. We drove to the ferry several kilometres south of the town and waited in the morning sun for it to sail. Four of my companions were previously acquainted—Liz and Antony from Liverpool, Dave and Lyn from London. They had worked in Sydney together in a Two Dollar Shop. Three others were siblings from south-east London: Sarah, Bill and Claire. The last was a quiet, slim woman from Bath, named Zoe, who had met the others a few days earlier. 'This better be worth it,' Antony muttered.

It took half an hour to reach the island. Liz joined me at the stern. Her freckled face beamed amiably. In the sunlight her auburn hair became a conflagration. 'Antony and I went to Kakadu on a tour, a small group like this. After we bonded we had a fabulous time.' Her smile revealed her optimism.

Antony begged to drive. He backed our vehicle onto the docking ramp, and we were soon travelling along a soft sandy track through lovely rainforest. One passenger sat in the front; the rest of us were in the back against the sides, squeezed between our packs, the camping equipment, food and alcohol. Antony was travelling fast, but the wheels were in such deep ruts the vehicle was in no danger of leaving the track. It bounced on the uneven surface, tossing us around on our seats like rag dolls. We raced through rainforest to Lake McKenzie, where the trees were less impressive. As we stepped out at the carpark, Antony inspected the vehicle. 'Seems to handle all right,' he said with sly pleasure.

Within five minutes another vehicle arrived in a spray of sand. The rear door sprang open and five young men jumped out. They began dancing around, flinging their heels and raising their knees, keeping a soccer ball aloft.

THE RED ISLAND

'What took you so long?' Antony cried.

Dave explained to me that a few of the soccer players were part owners of their van. 'I'm travelling with these mad bastards.'

I followed them through a picnic area to the lake. A skinny Irishman, who was with the soccer players, pointed to a sign. 'Look at that,' he said. '"No interacting with the dingoes." What the hell does that mean? I don't intend kissing the bleeding things.'

There was a stretch of beach around part of the lake. None of the Britons had seen sand so white. And the crystalline water mesmerised them. They stripped down to their bathers and sat on the sand and contemplated the prospect of swimming. The soccer players kept up their antics, taking advantage of the soft ground to develop new routines. They leapt and dived and headed wildly and eventually blundered into the lake. The first slab of beer was broken open. 'Look at that!' someone cried. 'A dingo.'

'Here's your chance, Eanon,' Liz said to the Irishman.

As a scrawny ginger dog slunk around some bushes nearby, they reached for their cameras. They started with the dingo and finished with photos of themselves living like Australians, lying around half-naked on a blinding bright beach doing nothing except drinking beer and having a good time.

After lunch, three of the soccer lads took the key of the second vehicle and disappeared. They bogged the vehicle, and we wasted an hour pulling it free. Then, heading for another lake, Antony took a wrong turn, and it was some time before we realised it. Disgruntled, he turned around and sped back, hunched over the wheel and glowering at each treacherous dip or hump in the track.

Lake Wabby was near the east coast. By the time we reached its carpark, the trees were casting long shadows across the ground. The other vehicle was there. We hurried

east coast

along a kilometre of rough walking track to a dark mere at the edge of a towering sand dune, where the soccer lads were skylarking and chortling like schoolboys and Eanon was smoking dope with his two female companions. 'What took you so long?' he said.

The sand was like a glacier, moving imperceptibly over the landscape, reducing the size of the lake by a couple of metres each year. I went for a long walk over the dune until I caught a glimpse of the sea. When I returned Antony was urging us to leave.

We had been given a map of Fraser Island at the hostel and warned to avoid tracks marked with a black felt pen. But the quickest way to the coast, where we hoped to camp, was along a black line. Antony drove down a steep track so badly eroded that the vehicle lurched and rolled like a drunk heading home. Tree roots protruding through the sandy surface partly blocked our path, and powdery pans threatened to steal our traction. Only the gradient and the law of gravity ensured we reached the beach. And what a contrast! Suddenly the terrain was flat and smooth, a long wide beach between the scrubby hills and the daunting ocean.

We stopped to wait for the other vehicle which wasn't far behind us. The siblings jumped out and ran towards the sea, scattering gulls which rose and baulked on the erratic air currents above the breakers. The constant roll of the sea muted the avian protests. Spray drifted, sharp and pure, across the beach. I took off my shoes, dug my bare feet into the sand, and breathed in the salubrious air.

'I'm so envious of you living in a country like this,' said Sarah, after she skipped over to me, her large chest heaving from the exertion of chasing her younger siblings into the waves. She was a brunette like her brother, while her sister was platinum blonde. 'I can't believe how many beautiful beaches you have. It's not fair.'

The soccer lads and company arrived. A conference took

THE RED ISLAND

place. And then we were back in the vehicles driving along the hard damp part of the beach looking for a suitable area of foreshore to camp. We had travelled about ten kilometres when we spotted a track through a gap in the low sandhills. A group of tents occupied a flat piece of land just beyond the gap, but the track continued behind the hills. A hundred and fifty metres further on we found enough space to camp.

Antony got out and stretched his legs. He waited until everyone milled around. 'This is all right,' he said. 'We're out of the wind. We've got a bit of company down there if anything goes wrong. We've still got enough light left to put our tents up and start a meal. So what are we waiting for? Let's get on with it.'

He was finishing his last sentence when I heard a low thumping sound—a shot of some sort. I looked up in time to see a projectile glance from the side of one of the vehicles and hit Antony. He clutched his ear and whimpered. The projectile bounced along the track a few times before falling into a depression in the sand. Nobody seemed to realise what had happened, least of all Antony. 'Who did that?' he cried accusingly, grasping his ear.

I picked up the projectile, an orange, and showed it to him. 'Someone from that campsite shot this at you, with a homemade bazooka or something,' I said.

Antony moaned. 'Who'd do a bloody thing like that?'

'Yobbos. Fishermen probably.'

Eanon came over. 'Now that's what I call a waste of good fruit.'

All the group gathered around. 'We can't stay here,' someone groaned. 'Who knows what could happen?'

'Why should we let a couple of fucking rednecks frighten us away?' said Smokey, one of the soccer lads. 'Let's just stay here. Fuck 'em.'

'Why don't you use your eyes?' another answered. 'There's more than a couple.'

east coast

'Ah, you coward. I'll go down there and tell 'em we're just a harmless lot of Pommies, and to leave off or face the fucking wrath of Britain.'

'And what do you have in mind, exactly?' said Eanon, putting his shaved head forward with a mocking grin. 'Throwing our watermelon at 'em?'

Indecision again plagued them. Suddenly I felt responsible for my compatriots' behaviour. 'Look, wait here,' I said rashly. 'I'll go down and speak to them.'

Nobody volunteered to accompany me. Smokey turned away and whistled at the moon emerging over the sand hills. It was a silent walk. The sand muffled my footsteps. None of the Britons larked around.

The campsite was still. I counted seven tents and as many vehicles, but could see nobody. I wondered what I was trying to prove. I glanced back at the Britons, who were all watching my progress. Ahead of me someone emerged from a tent and walked to the edge of the campsite. He looked in his thirties, a round-shouldered man, with the smile of a delinquent under his thick moustache. I said politely, 'Have you got a problem with us camping over there?'

He laughed defensively. 'No, matey, why?'

'I thought you might have, since someone here just shot at us.'

He switched his weight from one foot to the other and pushed his hands into the pockets of his jeans, unsettled I presumed by my politeness. 'No, no, wasn't us, matey.'

'If you don't want us camping there, tell us now and we'll move. That way you won't have to shoot at us again.'

'You can camp where you like. It's a free country.'

'That's what I thought.' I sealed our negotiations with a smile, then turned and walked back to the others, half-expecting an orange to smack into my skull.

The Britons were unconvinced there would be no more trouble, so we continued north for half an hour, until we saw

THE RED ISLAND

a flat rise amongst some melaleucas. We erected the tents, cooked in the dark and had a peaceful night. But it wasn't our last encounter with anglers.

In the morning, I rose early and woke the rest of the group. When the campsite was cleared, we headed up the long stretch of beach towards Indian Head. At low tide the beach became a highway. Dozens of four-wheel drive vehicles sped along the damp sand. Antony was still driving, still sullen. All along the water's edge, anglers held long rods that arched towards the surf.

We stopped at the village of Happy Valley to refuel and buy refreshments, and again at the rusted-out hulk of a beached ship where the Britons clambered about taking photos. It was a delightful day. The sun was shining. Sea birds glided on drafts above the waves. Dingoes lurked around. We passed Indian Head, one of the few stony outcrops on the island, and had lunch in a camping ground at Waddy Point.

The siblings and Zoe went over to a large tent to talk to some Australian men, who were on an angling holiday. They told them about the shooting incident. 'The tall guy apologised for his countrymen's behaviour,' said Zoe. 'He said he'd never heard of anything like that happening before.' They were lawyers from Brisbane who came to Fraser Island twice a year, once with their families and again for a 'boys only' fishing trip. 'Anyway, they invited themselves to our party tonight.'

We returned to a treeless area behind Indian Head where most of the sixty backpackers on the tour were camping. In the afternoon I climbed the outcrop to watch tiger sharks cruise around its rocky base and dolphins frolic in the breakers. The party that Zoe had mentioned was for Eanon, who claimed it was his birthday. He celebrated in his tent all afternoon, smoking dope with his two female companions.

Towards evening, we prepared a meal on a campfire. Fatigue had subdued most of the soccer boys. We sat around

east coast

quietly drinking. The siblings rolled out their sleeping bags and dozed.

'Hello, hello, hello! What's going on here?' cried one of the anglers from Waddy Point, appearing out of the darkness. 'It's a bloody quiet party, isn't it?'

'We're just mourning the passing of another year,' Eanon said. 'Show your respects, man.'

'Where's the fridge?' When he placed a carton of beer on the ground, there was a clamour of greetings. He scratched his silver beard, pleased with the reception. 'Sound like yers are dying of thirst.'

'You just added another few hours to the period of mourning,' Eanon said. 'And I'm not talking daylight hours here, you know, the time of day between breakfast and lunch. That's spelt different. But I suppose you Aussies wouldn't know that. I'm talking grief at the passing of another year.'

'You'd be Irish by the sounds of it,' said the fisherman.

'You're a clever man. What's your name?'

'Gary.'

'Oh, well, never mind. You can join us anyway.'

'So, it's a wake, not a party, eh? Well, I've heard the wakes in Ireland are better than the parties.' He dropped onto his haunches and pulled a can of beer from the carton. There were almost twenty tourists settled around the campfire. He looked around, his face looking churlish in the glow, and noticed we were eating. 'Did Zoe cook?'

'No, the boys did.'

'I'm tired,' Zoe mumbled, lying on her belly.

He tapped her on the shoulder. 'Are you having a good time? That's the main thing,' he said. 'The Australian hospitality is great, eh? I'd hate to think you went away thinking Aussie blokes were terrible.'

Zoe pulled the hair away from her face. 'We say "Fucking Aussies are shit" all the time. Generally.'

Gary laughed insincerely. 'Most Aussies are pretty good

57

THE RED ISLAND

blokes,' he said. 'There's a few vegetables.'

'Speaking of vegetables,' said Smokey. 'Here's one of your mates.'

'How's it going?' the other fisherman, a short Sri Lankan, asked Gary as he gave the scene a furtive glance.

'Yeah great, Snapper,' said Gary, passing him a can. 'Zoe's coming to clean our tent out tomorrow.'

Snapper leered at Zoe's tiny buttocks. 'Ah, Zoe, how are you?'

'Do your own cleaning,' she mumbled.

Snapper sat down close to her. 'We'd like to have you around,' he said.

Gary offered her a can. 'You look sad, Zoe,' he said. 'Got a problem?'

'Nothing you can help me with.'

'Sad affairs of the heart by the look of you.'

'We've all got problems,' muttered Smokey. 'It's getting fucking cold.'

I said, 'These people don't think Australians have got any problems.'

Sarah rose from her sleeping bag, wiped her eyes and looked at me. 'You have a better way of life.'

Gary put his hand on Snapper's neck and gave him a gentle shake. Snapper's eyes lulled. 'We don't have much to complain about,' Gary said. 'Nobody bothers anybody here. Everyone minds their own business and gets along fine. That's how it should be, don't yer reckon? There's a few idiots around, like whoever shot at you last night. But we go overseas and we see other countries, then we come back here and say we're lucky to be living here. And we've got the best beaches in the world. We're not bragging. Well, we are.'

Liz said, 'We all love our country. We think it's the best, too. But we'd all like to come here to live.'

---

east coast

The Britons' next stop, like most of the young backpackers on this coastal jaunt, was Airlie Beach, where they would take a cruise of the Whitsunday Islands. After that, it was Mission Beach to paraglide and shoot whitewater. I decided to postpone a trip to the Great Barrier Reef until I reached Cairns, and to stay at some places where the foreign tourists rarely stopped. Rockhampton, Bowen, Townsville.

In the late afternoon, I caught the bus for Rockhampton. I put earplugs in and watched the scenery. The sun was stretching the shadows of saplings across empty paddocks. A magpie followed an invisible path to its nest. By the time the coach reached the junction of the coastal road and Bruce Highway, I was drowsy.

I opened my eyes as we passed through a small town. In the twilight I could see that the advances of the late twentieth century had passed it by. Old timber houses on stilts, verandahs with posts along the main street, corrugated iron roofs. After travelling through hundreds of kilometres of slick urban development, I was pleased to see that a town like this had survived. It was from an era when small towns still had vitality, local jobs flourished, and a sense of community was solid. It reminded me that travelling the eastern seaboard gave a distorted impression of affluence while, not too far inland, rural towns throughout the country were slowly choking to death from economic torpor and the drift of people into cities.

I stared through the window, and set eyes on something that made me doubt my sanity. Two hundred metres away, running parallel to the highway, was a steam locomotive with several ageing carriages through whose open windows streamers, balloons and the faces of laughing old men appeared. Even from a distance they seemed to be waving at me. The streamers and balloons flapped madly in the draught. Suddenly the train disappeared—whether from my

THE RED ISLAND

imagination or behind a hill, I couldn't tell; night had stolen clarity.

I slept most of the way to Rockhampton, waking once as we passed through the industrial wastelands of Gladstone where I thought I spotted a road sign pointing to Sin Valley. Arriving at midnight I walked several blocks with my luggage to a hotel on the banks of the Fitzroy River. And in the morning, after a sound sleep, I went for a pleasurable stroll along the riverfront and around the city centre.

Many of the buildings in Rockhampton, like the hotel, dated back to the nineteenth century. The post office in the East Street Mall, the old Customs House with its Corinthian columns and lofty dome, and the offices of maritime companies and the cattlemen's association by the wide river were still in fine condition. But in old residential streets where weatherboard houses were raised on stilts, shutters were closed and paint peeled from the external walls, mimicking the shabby character of dwellings I'd seen around the Caribbean. The air was warm and palms outnumbered eucalypts. Rockhampton, the centre of the Queensland cattle industry, was astride the Tropic of Capricorn.

There were some Aboriginals in the mall. They were thin, dark-skinned people in shabby clothes. They looked sad and uncertain. I watched them talking in small groups in a nasal English. Whites in the street avoided passing near them or stared through them as if they didn't exist. They seemed like strangers in their own town. Curious to find out if they were actually locals I stopped one of them as he walked past. He was a shy man and he talked so quietly I couldn't understand him.

I spent the morning sitting by the river, reading, and writing letters. It was already August. I had been travelling for almost six weeks. I missed Tania. I was beginning to wish that she had accompanied me. She was the perfect person to travel with, garrulous and inquisitive. An unsuccessful

east coast

encounter with a shy Aboriginal would not have discouraged her. In a local newspaper, I discovered that the train I had seen the previous evening was real. It was the Australia Remembers Troop Train, 'a commemorative re-enactment of the World War II troop transports', due in Rockhampton at 4 p.m. on its trip from Brisbane to Townsville for the Victory in the Pacific Day celebrations. I was inclined to scoff at displays of military pomp, like the parade of tanks at the start of my trip. But I decided to go to the railway station to watch it arrive.

I walked in the wrong direction, turned back, and eventually crossed a railway track that ran down the middle of a street. The temperature was in the mid-twenties, but it was humid, and I felt uncomfortably sticky and slightly disorientated. I went into a pub, and sat on a stool where I could see the railway through the door. 'I suppose I'll see the diggers' train from here,' I said to the barmaid, who looked up from the game of euchre she was playing on the bar with an old emaciated alcoholic, her only customer. She pouted sceptically.

'It's coming from the other direction,' her opponent said without lifting his eyes from his cards.

'Well, I might as well have a beer while I'm here,' I said. 'I've been walking around in the heat looking for the station.'

'Heat?' the barmaid muttered as she served me. She wore a cardigan buttoned over her fat belly. 'It's bloody freezing. You ought to stand here in this draught all day, and then tell me it's hot.' She angled her head towards the open door.

'It's quiet around here.' I looked around the bar, which had the usual decor—posters with buxom women in rugby jumpers, caricatures of dogs playing pool—and the usual sour smells.

'Meatworks haven't been working, have they, Charlie?'

'Eight months,' he responded. 'Lot of trouble.' He slapped a card on the bar.

THE RED ISLAND

'Strikes?'

'Nah.' He threw down his last card and picked up his tin of tobacco. 'Lock out.'

'There was a lot of strikes,' the barmaid corrected. 'But they're going to open again soon. One of them has changed hands.'

Charlie ran his tongue along the glue on his cigarette paper. He finished the ritual with a subtle roll of his fingers and stuck the result to his bottom lip. He lit his cigarette with a match, then puffed on it until the coughing began. He lifted himself off his stool, put the tobacco tin in his pocket, waved breathlessly at the barmaid and shuffled towards the door.

'Righto, Charlie, see yer tomorrow,' she called.

The barmaid began to clean up the slops. 'You've lived here all your life, have you?' I ventured.

'Long enough,' she muttered. 'Listen, if yer want to catch that train, yer better get your arse into gear.'

With so much Victorian architecture in Rockhampton, I expected to find a grand railway station. But the building was modern, functional and bland. The long platform was crowded with people of all ages. A school brass band played while four armed teenagers in fatigues and slouch hats formed a guard of honour near the exit. I pushed my way through the cheerful gathering from one end of the platform to the other, but the only medals I saw were on the hound-stooth jacket of a young man, who had sunglasses clamped like a headband over his blond hair and an unusually tall woman linked to his arm. He stopped to chat with an elderly man whose eyes were level with the woman's tanned cleavage. She enjoyed the attention, swaying forward a little for his benefit, sucking alternately on a menthol cigarette and a lolly pop.

Over the sounds of the band, a station worker announced that the train was only minutes away. When the first hiss of steam billowed under the platform awning, hundreds of little

east coast

Australian flags appeared in the waving hands of onlookers. The band greeted the diggers with a rousing tune. As two coupled steam engines pulled the carriages into the station, the old soldiers in civilian clothes leaned out of windows beaming gratefully. Streamers and balloons, fluttering flags, the shouts of hoorah, a formal military welcome, the anachronistic atmosphere, the memories. It was too much for the old woman standing next to me. She swayed a little and, as I steadied her, she emitted a long melancholic fart.

After an overnight stop in Rockhampton, the train was heading for Mackay and Bowen before it arrived in Townsville on Victory in the Pacific Day. I intended to pass through Mackay and stay a night in Bowen. I'd beat the train to Townsville. While the diggers disembarked, I strolled down to take a closer look at the locomotives, to admire their crude ingenuity.

The lead engine was green and black, a hissing barrel held together with huge rivets and bolts. Pipes of various diameters ran over its surface like protruding arteries. Steel piston rods extended from their cylinder housings to the gleaming wheels. I asked a middle-aged man in a railway uniform and an old couple dressed in their Sunday bests if they knew whether it was an original troop train. The railway man pulled at the peak of his cap. 'Oh, yeah,' he said. 'Go on board and you'll find old Blamey himself.'

The sartorial old fellow left the side of his wife and came over. 'This old lady's a beauty. They don't make trains like this any more.'

'Closest thing man's made to an animal,' said the railway man.

The old man's wife joined us, adjusting her pink cardigan. 'My brother-in-law used to drive one and he says they're alive. They've got personalities.' She ran her gaze along its flanks and sighed. 'Oh, they're wonderful.'

'Beautiful!' added her husband. 'Of course, I mightn't say

THE RED ISLAND

that if I had to shovel coal into her. What a lovely old lady!'

I asked the railway worker if he'd travelled on the troop train during the war. He gave a buck-toothed smile and blushed. 'They wanted me in an armaments factory down in Brisbane,' he confessed.

'They haven't kept enough of 'em,' said the other fellow. 'You know the Swedes have got the right idea. They've buried a number of 'em deep in the mountains. They won't say how many. It's a military secret. But they've got the right idea. We should be doing it, too. I don't like this dependency on oil. Can't trust the Arabs, you know.'

'It's the end of an era,' said his wife.

'It may not be. The day might come when we need it again.'

I excused myself and thanked them. 'I've got to go,' I said.

The old fellow gave me an understanding nod. 'Never met a steam man who wasn't a great yapper,' he said.

———

The countryside north of Rockhampton was ravaged by drought. Listless white Brahmin cattle, whose ribs cast shadows like zebra stripes along their flanks, foraged for withered blades of grass around strange small helical trees. There was bare dirt between the road and the few strands of barbed wire containing the cattle. In the distance, the unobtrusive range that stretched, unbroken, along the east of Australia looked cruelly like rain clouds. I saw the crude frames of abandoned sheds but no other signs of human occupation.

We passed through Marlborough and, hours later, Sarina, where the dry scrub ended and the sugar plantations began. They stretched inland away from its pungent refinery. The air was viscous. And for the next few hours the road was a shimmering green corridor, broken only by murky water channels and narrow-gauge rails for sugar-cane locomotives.

east coast

We passed through Mackay, the sugar port, and detoured into Airlie Beach, a crush of hotels and bars along a rocky piece of coast. For much of the trip a Canadian girl drowsed on my shoulder. Whenever I looked through the window the mountain range was a different distance from the highway. At times it had substance—crags of sheer rock with crevices of captured soil and vegetation—but more often it was a smudge on the horizon, cloudlike. The sugar cane ended, and the countryside became scrubby, cut by eroded creeks, until mango orchards signalled the proximity of Bowen.

I caught sight of the town over hills of salt and evaporation pools. The rusting stack of an old coke works made it easy to pinpoint. But by the time I'd left the bus and walked around several blocks searching for accommodation, nothing except the stack looked familiar. The locals wore baseball caps and runners, and drove four-wheel drives. Both hostels were full and in each hotel I entered I got the same laconic rejection. Harvest workers had occupied every available room in town. I walked down to the waterfront to look for a possible shelter for the night. There was a port of sorts—a pier that divided like a fork into wharves where a couple of large tug boats were moored. The wind was whipping the sea into froth and bending the palm trees towards the town. I scouted around but found no shelter where I could doss down overnight. I sat for a while, leaning against my pack. Then I saw a car towing a van along the foreshore road. I picked up my pack and hurried in the direction it was taking.

The manager of the caravan park squinted suspiciously at me and said he had no overnight vans available. My heart sank. 'Not unless you can pay for it,' he added.

'Of course!' I almost shouted in relief.

I woke late the following morning, had breakfast in the van, then took my luggage to the travel bureau. I had several hours to wait for the bus, so I returned to the shore. The tide was low. Waders, both the feathered and gumbooted

THE RED ISLAND

varieties, poked at the beach for buried molluscs. Out on the pier I met a young angler, Paul Watson, who came marching past me with his father's new fishing line. 'It's the first time he's let me use it,' he declared.

He looked twelve or thirteen. 'Where is he?' I asked.

'He's at work.' His father picked and his mother and sisters sorted tomatoes on a farm near Bowen. He lived with them at the caravan park. He didn't go to school. 'I'm fifteen,' he grinned. 'And I got all the legal papers. I don't have to go any more.' He lifted his baseball cap to scratch his sandy head, then strolled ahead in his broken runners.

'Don't you work with them?' I asked, catching up to him.

'Sometimes. But I'm fishing today. Yesterday I caught eight herring.'

'What did you do with them?'

'Ate 'em.'

'You couldn't eat eight.'

'Big family. Eight sisters plus mum and dad.' Today he wanted to catch a shark like the one his father caught recently. 'Five foot,' he said, using the imperial measurement of his father's generation. 'I caught a groper once. I didn't think I was going to get him in. He nearly broke off before I could gaff him. I had to carry him along the beach. I was like this.' He bent over to mimic his trip home with the groper. 'See that hook? That's a gang hook.'

'Looks vicious,' I said.

'It is, man. It's for catching more than one fish.'

I followed him along the timber pier, past where it divided and became the tugboat wharf. On the pier there were other anglers. Peter made a quick tour of inspection to find out what was biting, then chose a position in the sheltered water between the pier and wharf. He showed me how to cut the head off a bream, which he was using for bait, so the knife didn't go blunt on the bone. 'Where do your mum and dad work when the tomato season finishes?'

east coast

'We pick grapes and oranges down Renmark way,' he said, without looking up from his preparations. 'Sometimes we do pears round Shepparton in Victoria.'

'You've got a caravan, I suppose.'

'Mobile home,' he corrected proudly. 'Me dad shifts it with the old prime mover he's done up. Me mum drives the Commodore.'

'How do you like the life? You don't get sick of the travel?'

He looked at me as if I were crazy. 'You wouldn't catch me living in no city, that's for sure.'

'What about friends?'

'I got me family, haven't I? Anyway, look round here. All these blokes'll talk to yer.'

I went off to chat to another fisherman for a while. When I returned to see how Peter was doing, his line was dangling in the water, but he was on the other side of the pier, studying a flathead that someone else had just caught. 'How's the shark hunt going?' I asked.

He cantered back to his line and began to reel it in. 'What shark?' he said. 'I'm after flathead.'

Seated next to me as I left Bowen was a man named Warren. When he told me he was a dancer, I wasn't surprised. His hair was cut fashionably short at the sides. His haughty poise alluded to some classical training. He was a partner in an Aboriginal dance company that worked all across Australia—at theatres, schools, town halls, festivals. 'I dance modern and traditional,' he said. Warren's eyes seldom turned from the landscape. He was on his way to Yarrabah Aboriginal community near Cairns to ask permission from an uncle to perform a particular dance. The traditional dances he knew belonged to his five

THE RED ISLAND

blood lines, including some from his father's family who lived on a Torres Strait island. To ensure he understood these dances and to avoid their corruption, he always consulted his elders before he performed them.

When I asked him if he had been brought up learning other traditions, he said, 'My father taught me how to spear, both on land and for fishing.' He had caught turtle but never a dugong. 'Dugongs cry tears and wail when they're caught. You have to have a strong heart to kill one.' He told me that whenever his mother chastised him he would run away into the bush for days and live off the land. When he started to feel guilty about his behaviour he returned. 'But I always put on weight living on bush tucker.'

'What about crocs?' I asked. 'You see many of them in the rivers?'

He had seen some at Yarrabah. 'You have to respect them,' he said. 'Have you got a mobile phone?' He laughed and told me about two fishermen who had recently been chased up a tree by a crocodile but were able to phone for help because one of them had a mobile.

It was dark when we reached Townsville, one of Queensland's major cities. I said goodbye to Warren as he stood looking despondently at the choice of food in steamy trays at the bus terminal's cafeteria.

—————

Townsville, which had a large army base, was full of visitors for Victory in the Pacific, VP50 Day celebrations, people from all over Australia and the South Pacific. Face-painted islanders in floral wraparounds and grass skirts walked the corridors of the hostel where I was staying.

None of them was billeted in my dormitory. Instead there was an old eccentric German, and two Australians. One had a Buffalo Bill mane and goatee. When he first arrived in the

68

east coast

dormitory, he mumbled something incomprehensible. Nobody responded. 'Thanks for the fucking greeting,' he said. He slung himself onto an upper bunk and lay fully clothed staring at the ceiling while I sorted through my pack. 'Wake me in an hour,' he commanded and promptly fell asleep. I went to the laundry and when I returned his hour was up. I called him but he failed to stir. I shook him.

'Was I dreaming?' He sat up, startled.

'I don't know.'

'Why did you fucking wake me then?'

'You asked me to,' I said impatiently. He sprang from the bunk and began sorting through a small bag of possessions. His insubstantial luggage and lack of bedding prompted me to ask if he actually lived in Townsville.

'No, man, I'm from somewhere else.'

'Just passing through?'

'I've got a job as a marshal for the VP50 Day celebrations.'

'Good money?'

'I'm not after money.' He stopped his search to focus his fervent eyes on me. 'I'm trying to understand my father.' He got to his feet abruptly and hurried from the room.

He returned later in the night and went to bed, again fully dressed and without a cover. I slept lightly, with my valuables at the bottom of my sleeping sheet. The moment he started shouting my eyes shot open. I didn't move. 'You cunt!' he cried. 'I'll fucking knock your head off!' He was lying on his bed addressing phantoms. 'Why ask me, cunt?' He smashed his fist into the brick wall next to his bunk.

In the morning, tired and nervous, I went for a long walk around Townsville, past Castle Hill, the bald outcrop behind the city centre that an obstinate local had decided to raise to the official height of a mountain by dumping barrow loads of dirt on it. Down to The Strand where banyan trees were anchored to the foreshore. Along Ross Creek, a stinking inlet

THE RED ISLAND

for fishing fleets, leisure craft, and the ferries that serviced Magnetic Island, eight kilometres offshore.

The island seemed the perfect place to restore my peace of mind. So I took the ferry across to Picnic Bay and a bus to a quiet village on the far side that faced the open sea. The warm sun and breakfast were just the remedy I needed. Later, I found a track and hiked into the hills where the bush was drier and hotter than the coast. Then I strolled down the eastern slopes to Arcadia on Alma Bay. By the time I had rounded two points the weather was changing. Clouds swept across the mainland and the sea had become choppy.

On the sandy foreshore at Nelly Bay I met Gaba, a Papua New Guinea man, looking anxiously at the weather. His grey fuzzy hair swept off his forehead in the wind, and his dark bloodshot eyes moved from one end of the cloud bank to the other. Before him, half-beached on the shore, was the boat he had assembled from cedar logs, cross beams and rigging. Rolled up on the beach next to him was a huge sail woven from reeds. The boat was a lagatoi, and further along the bay a second one was beached.

'The timber was brought here from Papua New Guinea,' he said, rubbing his fat belly exposed between a windcheater and brown wraparound. 'We're going to sail them across to Townsville on Sunday. Part of the VP50 Day celebrations.' Small red flags and reeds along the mast stays flapped furiously in the wind. 'We're worried about this weather. If it keeps up we won't be able to cross. We need the wind behind us.'

'Were lagatois used in the war?'

'No. They're just a gift of friendship from Papua New Guinea.'

'What do you use them for?'

'To trade sago along the coast and up the rivers.'

'So you live a traditional life?'

'I'm a retired car salesman,' he said with a faint smile,

east coast

exposing teeth that were stained with betel juice. 'I live in a house that sits over the water on a river near Port Moresby. I have a dinghy and a vegetable garden, enough to live on. You go after too much money, you only get problems.'

The weather appeared to be holding. I hitchhiked to Picnic Bay and took a rough ferry ride back to Townsville.

Preparations for VP50 Day were evident in the city. A huge replica of the Victory sign, attached to the railway station facade at the end of World War II, had been installed. Scores of tables were set for a banquet in the Town Hall plaza. Crowds gathered in the streets to watch a parade—perhaps a rehearsal for the next day's commemoration—of military bands. And in the evening, fireworks exploded amongst the multi-storeyed buildings, sounding like the return of war. I went to the hostel to check that Buffalo Bill hadn't broken into my rucksack, ate a small pizza at the bus terminal cafeteria, then crossed the street to have a drink in a rowdy pub.

One stool was vacant at the bar. I squeezed onto it and found myself next to a dour short-bearded man whose fists guarded a glass of whisky. When I greeted him, he ignored me. 'Do you mind if I sit here?' I persisted. I noticed his jaw muscles twitch. 'You don't want to speak? That's your prerogative.' I said, trying to sound cheerful.

'You're fucking bald,' he muttered without looking at me.

'You noticed? I'm flattered.'

'Agent orange?'

'Agent orange?' I struggled to comprehend the connection. 'No, mate, old age.'

'Old age? What do you mean?' He turned his head without moving his shoulders and narrowed his eyes. 'How old are you?'

'Forty-three.'

'You call that old? Christ, I've got to say it, you look fucking ugly. Look at those fucking ears. You believe in

THE RED ISLAND

science fiction? You've got ears from outer space.'

'I'm not asking you to kiss me.'

'Are you some kind of killer? You're ugly enough for it.' When I ignored him he added, 'You think that worries me? It don't. I'm a Green Beret.'

'Is that so?' I wanted to sound unimpressed, but my voice betrayed me. Besides, I was momentarily confused. I thought Green Berets were American, but my tormentor had an Australian accent.

Someone nudged my shoulder. I turned around, half expecting to find another Green Beret seated on the other side. Instead a blotchy face smiled at me—an Irishman, I gathered, once he opened his mouth. 'Don't take that sort of shit from him,' he advised. His thin moist lips drew back tightly until his cheeks looked ready to bloom. He raised a finger unsteadily as if he were about to make another point but changed his mind. The finger wavered and returned to the bar.

'It's all right,' I said, alarmed by his tactlessness. 'We're just having a friendly chat.'

'Just talk to me. Don't take any notice of this empty-headed loafer.' His eyelids drooped as he nodded at the Green Beret. 'Excuse me, but nature's calling.'

He suddenly left me alone with the Green Beret, who was missing my company, apparently. 'Look I'm sorry. You can't help how ugly you are,' he said. 'What is it, cancer? Is that why you're bald?'

'Look, mate, I like being bald. I like the way I look. I like the ears. I don't have a problem with it. So I don't see why you're trying to make it yours.'

Something had sapped Green Beret's aggression. 'I was in Vietnam. I'm searching for something, man. What life is about,' he said. He tried to order another whisky, but the barman refused to serve him. He stood up, put on a Marines baseball cap and angled its peak proudly. He picked up his

72

east coast

overnight bag from the floor and stood behind me for an unnerving moment before leaving.

———

I decided to leave VP50 Day, Buffalo Bill and Green Beret behind. I wanted a change of scenery. And the change was dramatic. If only for a moment in the coach, after the highway left the coastal plain and climbed into the mountains a couple of hours from Townsville, I caught sight of the loveliest vista in Queensland: a serpentine channel of glistening sea between mangroves on the coast and Hinchinbrook Island. North from here the land was steamy and verdant, an immense tropical garden that stretched along the coast for another thousand kilometres to the tip of Cape York. Before we reached Tully, diurnal rain was falling in lethargic drops, rising immediately as steam from the shining road. It rained all the way to Cairns.

———

Thanks to Japanese tourism, Cairns had doubled its size in two decades. Immaculately dressed tourists wandered the city's shopping centre. Signs were in Japanese. Shop staff spoke Japanese. Opals and toy koalas competed with dot paintings and didgeridoos for yen. The entire city centre had been modified to make its foreign guests feel at home.

A few old ghosts wandered around—bearded, tattooed, barefoot men in soiled singlets and shorts who sat in pubs staring lugubriously through slatted windows at modern Cairns. One of them sat next to me on a bench in City Place Mall. He was a small fellow whose hair beneath a leather cap was turning white. 'How are you?' I asked.

'Apart from the cancer in my hip,' he said. 'I've got this gut ache or soreness in my side.' He pressed it and grimaced.

THE RED ISLAND

'I had my gall bladder out. I had six stones this big.' He indicated the size of marbles. 'I've just seen my doctor. Ah, he's good, old Bert. He says I'm going to die of the same thing as Errol Flynn. Sex and drugs.'

'The hard living, huh?'

'The hard living,' he repeated sentimentally. 'It caught up with me.'

'How long have you lived in Cairns then?'

He smiled and sighed. 'Longer than I care to remember.'

'Changed a lot, has it?'

'It's hardly recognisable. This shop here, that cafe, the Italian cobbler down there, they're the only three originals left. I could've sat here ten years ago and I'd have known every second person who came along. Now I might be lucky to see one if I sat all day.' Nevertheless, in the next fifteen minutes three people greeted him. He called one, a young woman, 'pumpkin'; another he told me was a 'cowboy' and the third an old drinking partner who didn't often come to town these days.

In some respects the popularity of Cairns as a tourist destination surprised me. It was a reasonable departure point for the trips to the Great Barrier Reef, but not the only one. It had a scenic railway that climbed the Atherton Tableland escarpment to Kuranda—perhaps the most enjoyable in Australia now that the north coast passenger service in Tasmania no longer operated. But Kuranda, once an idyllic village surrounded by rainforest, had been transformed into a tourist carnival. And Cairns, despite its image as a tropical paradise, had no beaches to speak of. From five-star hotels along the Esplanade the view was of mud flats extending for hundreds of metres at low tide, a boon for birdwatchers who would find no more convenient place in northern Queensland to observe ibises, egrets, sandpipers, knots, greenshanks, pelicans and curlews, but hardly the postcard vista of hot white sand with fringes of coconut palms. (It was a good twenty-minute drive

east coast

north to a useable beach.) Indeed, the land on the far side of the estuary, where the mountains sloped down to the sea, looked more enchanting. But I was projecting my own priorities onto others. And after I had walked around the city, observing recent developments—the casino, the opulent shopping complex called the Pier, the restaurants at Trinity Wharf—I had to remind myself that, for most tourists, spending money was as enjoyable as scenery.

I wanted to take a cruise out to the Barrier Reef but the weather for the next few days was unseasonably wet and windy. Storm after storm blew in from the south. Instead I caught a local bus to Gordonvale, a small sugar-mill town, where, by chance, I met Ranjit Singh and his son, Gurinder, two local Sikhs who worked at the mill. When I expressed an interest in seeing their temple, which I had noticed from the bus, they invited me to their home and patiently answered my questions about their religion and community.

'From Mackay to Mossman we are only sixty families,' Gurinder Singh said. He was a young man with a full black beard. Apart from the turban his clothes were quite ordinary—jeans and striped casual shirt. 'In Brisbane we are two hundred families.'

His father had a small face and a wiry body. His beard was streaked with grey. He apologised for his English. He had only been in Australia nine years. In India he had been a farmer, and his native language was Punjabi; it was hard for an old man to learn a new language fluently. 'With our hard work and honesty we put our roots very deep,' he said. 'I think Australia is the most peaceful country in the world. People know their rights. And it's a small population in a big country. The government doesn't interfere with people who have different religions. Here we have good ties with our neighbours and the local people.'

For the next hour Ranjit Singh told me about his religion, its history and philosophy, then he asked his son to take

THE RED ISLAND

me to their Gurdwara. It was an elegant temple with white cupolas and a golden arcade. I covered my head and took off my shoes before I stepped into an uncluttered room with a simple altar for its holy books and portraits of the Gurus on the walls. Gurinder Singh told me there was no priest. A member of one of the Sikh families came each day to open the doors, and each Sunday there were prayers. But every Sikh was capable of performing religious ceremonies. 'In the Gurdwara,' said Gurinder Singh, 'everyone is equal.'

———

Back in Cairns, I moped around the town waiting for the weather to improve so that I could take the dirt road, which was impassable in the wet, along the coast to Cooktown. Skid-row Aboriginals loitered in town like the nemesis of the tourist trade. They greeted me, as they greeted other whites, with 'Hello brother'. If I sat down near them in the mall they would come over to chat. 'The drink's got me,' one said, as if speaking for them all. 'I'm sick, brother. I can't beat it.' Occasionally they would ask for money, but it was never serious begging.

I talked to a cyclist who had ridden to one of the hostels at Cape Tribulation to the north of Cairns. I asked him if there was still a hippie community in the area. He remembered seeing some 'ferals'. 'Especially female ones who went swimming in the raw,' he added. 'The only time they ever wash. It got me, though, how they arrived at the hostel every night to watch *The Simpsons*. Their tree houses in the forest don't come with electricity, apparently.'

One morning I went to buy a paper and found the newsagent tossing magazines around. 'What a lot of crap!' he said, pointing at the displays around him. 'See there. They're all crap.' His vehemence made me chuckle. He followed me to the counter. His jowls were red with indignation.

76

east coast

'Ninety per cent of what you read in these is bullshit. What do we read it for?'

'How do we find out what's happening in the world?'

'What do you need to know? Not this! Who writes it? Journalists!' He ironed his blond moustache with his fingers. His eyes bulged. 'Have you ever a met a journalist? They can't lie straight in bed, the mongrels. They talk about the information age. I tell you, we're going to be overloaded with information soon and ninety per cent of it will be garbage. The superhighway will be so crammed with bullshit no-one will know what to believe. I'm telling you if JC knocked on this door today and said, "I've come to save the world" people would slam the door in his face.' He shook his head. 'No, we could all do without this.'

'But you'd be without a job,' I said, with a touch of malice.

'Maybe that'd be a good thing. Why work so hard? You just work to buy those things you don't need. You get a swimming pool installed, and you think "Wow!" But you find out it's just another bloody problem. I'm telling you, when the superhighway gets here, we're going to need another day in each week.'

'And what would you call it?'

'Crapday!'

I left the newsagency, walked straight to the bus terminal at Trinity Wharf, and booked a ticket for Cooktown.

The coast to Port Douglas was variable. Rock flows interrupted white beaches. Eucalypts covered any area too dry for rainforest. The only constant was the fervid blue expanse of sea and adjoining sky. With an improvement in the weather, the first calm day in a week, the trip promised to be pleasant.

The road wound through the hills never far from the shore. Within an hour we were in Port Douglas, a town that

THE RED ISLAND

in the eighties had grown from a few beach cottages, pub and store to a large resort. Twenty kilometres further on was Mossman, a sugar cane town, where we stopped to transfer into a sturdy all-terrain bus. Sugar plantations extended towards the Daintree River. We passed through a forest, and crossed several creeks that were apparently the habitats of crocodiles. When we passed Barrot Creek, the driver said, 'That's where that woman got taken a few years ago.'

We picked up more passengers at the Daintree village, then went to the ferry landing where two girls and an American tourist went searching for a toilet. We were mid-stream on the wide river before someone realised that they were still midstream elsewhere. 'That's the worst of them Woolworths bladders,' said the passenger in a towelling hat. 'I suppose we'll have to wait for 'em.'

When the ferry made its next crossing the trio rejoined us, and we set off through semi-cleared country where Brahmin cattle grazed up to their flanks in lush grass. Then we entered a rainforest that diffused the glare of the open land. As the road wound through a low range of hills, I could see the damage its construction had caused. Erosion had weakened the trees near the edges and many of them had toppled. The surface was crudely gouged by run-off. We travelled behind Mount Hutchinson then descended to the coast and followed the shore for another ten kilometres to Cape Tribulation.

The hostels and lodges at the cape were surrounded by jungle. Creepers dangled between the trees. Umbrella palms drooped listlessly under drips of water. The shoes of alighting passengers squelched on the soft ground.

I kept my eyes open, but didn't see any ferals, not even on the pieces of beach I occasionally glimpsed. The driver made a few quick stops, then returned to the road to Bloomfield. We forded a number of creeks and crossed the Cowie Range, went down a switchback to a dry river bed where the vegetation changed to scrub, then we crossed

east coast

another range to the Bloomfield River.

Although a concrete ford had been laid across the river, one section had been washed away. The driver told us he had been unable to cross on his previous attempt a few days earlier. But the water had dropped since then, and he drove into the rapid flow without hesitation.

Bloomfield was perched above the river, a few makeshift stores and modest dwellings. We drove on for an hour, past the Lion's Den, a hotel built from corrugated iron, until, close to the junction of the Bloomfield track and the inland road to Cooktown, we passed Black Mountain.

It was an extraordinary site, a towering pile of giant boulders blackened by lichen, a mountain of rubble that looked like it would tumble with the removal of any lower rock. Transfixed by its mystery and menace, I wasn't surprised to hear the driver say that people had lost their lives climbing amongst its boulders, trying to find a way through to the other side. The road skirted around it then twisted the other way until it was out of sight. Within half an hour we had crossed the Annon River, passed another range of hills, and arrived at Cooktown.

Several of its commercial buildings dated back to the Palmer River gold rush in the 1870s, when the town was an important port with a population of thirty thousand. When the gold rush ended Cooktown went into steady decline, until, by the end of World War II, it was almost a ghost town. Currently it had a population of about fifteen hundred.

I booked into a hostel on Charlotte Street and went for a stroll along a path near the river to the spot where, amongst the mangroves, Captain Cook had beached the *Endeavour* in 1770. Across the wide estuary, a white line of sandhills stretched northwards to a hilly headland. Behind it the land was wilderness.

During the two months it took to repair the damage that a nearby reef had done to his barque, Captain Cook had

THE RED ISLAND

climbed the knoll at the mouth of the river and with a yeoman's eyes despaired at what he saw: 'The low land near the river is wholly over-run with mangroves among which salt-water flows with every tide; and the high land appears to be every where stony and barren.' He made tentative contact with local Aboriginals and rather wistfully observed that without possessions, conveniences, and social inequalities they seemed far happier than Europeans.

The Aboriginals I saw in Cooktown seemed inconsolably miserable. They hung around town in small groups. Some went to pubs, where they were confined to squalid bars set aside for their use. They drank, played pool and occasionally brawled, much the same as the local whites. But their presence was generally resented. The prevailing sentiment in town seemed to be that government handouts had ruined them.

Later in the evening I met Pete, a bikie, at one of the squalid bars. He had ratty blond hair, a short beard and blue eyes. 'Let's get down to some serious drinking,' he said. He looked around at the Aboriginals playing pool. 'If you're new in town,' he reminded himself rather than advised me, 'never start a fight with someone in a pub, unless you know the other one's new too.'

'Where have you come from?' I asked.

'Northern Territory. I just left there a few days ago. Came across through Normanton. In the dust.' He laughed proudly at his achievement. We decided to walk to another pub to eat. 'It's a long time since I've been with a good woman,' he lamented after we had ordered. 'Too long. Shit, look at that chick over there. See her? Fucking five stars there, man.'

I looked around. 'Who?'

'That Asian chick, for Christ's sake!' There was a young

80

east coast

Filipino woman sitting with an middle-aged man. 'You know, when I was in Indonesia, you saw that bloody everywhere.' He shook his head in disbelief. 'These old white blokes with gorgeous Asian chicks hangin' off their arms.'

'Have you travelled anywhere else?'

'My dream trip, man. India on a motorbike,' he said and took a long swig of whisky. 'I flew to Bombay and bought a Royal Enfield, and began travelling around.'

'A Royal Enfield? Jesus, what a classic! I love those old bikes.'

'They're a dime a dozen over there, as common as fuckin' Hondas,' he said. 'It was wonderful, man, until I ran over a bloke in a village.' One of his eyes squinted at me. He drank more whisky. 'I nearly got killed by the crowd. They wanted my fuckin' blood.'

'What happened?'

'A four-wheel drive pulled up, driven by an educated man, thank Christ. He got me and the bloke I ran over into his car and took us to the nearest hospital.'

'The bloke you hit was all right, then?'

'He died in my arms.'

By the time our meals arrived my appetite had waned. But Pete had ordered barramundi and nothing was going to spoil his meal. 'I was thrown in jail on a manslaughter charge,' he said, pulling at the fish with his fork. 'I'd still be there if I hadn't paid a two thousand bucks bribe. I got a false passport and went straight to the nearest fuckin' airport and flew out of there.'

'What about the Royal Enfield?'

'Never saw it again. Nor India for that matter, man. If I went back they'd lock me up and throw away the fuckin' key.'

A German who was staying at the hostel arrived for a meal. He had hair like Art Garfunkel. He told us that three women had just booked in. 'One of them was also German,' he added happily.

THE·RED ISLAND

'How do you rate her?'

'Rate her?' Pete asked.

'Three stars? Four stars? You know, like the hotels, man.'

'Oh,' the German said, nodding. 'Definitely three stars.'

Pete considered it. 'That's all right,' he said. Wanting to get back to the hostel to meet them, he hurried through his meal. He washed down the barramundi with beer and wiped his cracked lips with a paper serviette. 'Let's go,' he said to me. 'We'll leave the German here.'

When we arrived at the hostel the only person in the recreation room was the owner, a nervous type who chain-smoked. 'Where's the new talent?' Pete demanded. 'I heard a German chick arrived tonight.'

'They've all gone to bed.'

'Without me?' Pete cried. He dropped onto an old divan. 'The only sex I've had recently was with a fuckin' scrubber.'

I went to bed and in the morning climbed Grassy Hill, where Cook and his botanist Joseph Banks had surveyed the land and through a telescope had seen natives lighting fires on the far shore, 'for what purpose we could not guess'—an incomprehension that still echoed through this land. In a pensive mood, I walked down a track to a small deserted beach and walked along its golden sand.

The morning was balmy but by mid-afternoon a change had swept in from the south. I was back in Cooktown near the wharf when the rain started. Ducking under a shelter attached to a canteen I ordered a coffee and sat to watch the rain creep across the estuary. I wasn't alone. At the next table a beefy man, in khaki shorts and Akubra hat, was informing two elderly tourists about the problems facing hard-working whites on Cape York, who were about to lose their pastoral leases with the declaration of a new national park to be managed by a local Aboriginal community. 'What a waste of bloody money!' he said, shaking his head.

'That's what we think, too.' The woman who spoke sat

east coast

erect in a blue summer skirt, her grey hair in a tight bun and rimless glasses perched low on her long nose. 'Isn't it, Charles?' Her husband, who was round-shouldered and portly, nodded. 'All these public works being done for the Abos, but they don't pay rates or anything.' She puckered her lips in thought.

'And I think it's so because the Aboriginal people in the last twenty-five years have lost their pride,' said the man in the Akubra. He shook his head, as if he were genuinely concerned. 'The government is just giving 'em money and they've got no motivation to do anything. The older blacks can't understand it. They worked bloody hard on the stations. I know. I was there when they were doing it. They used to be good hard-working people. Now they're all bloody alcoholics, funded by the government.'

'The stations used to give the blackfellas work,' said the woman. 'And rations, and somewhere for their wives and kids to live.'

'Yep.'

'I know all this because I had a friend who had a pastoral lease in the West. She had to stop her children doing housework because that was Aboriginal women's work. And she had to tell them not to go down to the camp. It's not right, is it, for white kiddies to mix with blacks?' She tutted and looked at her husband, whose head was bowed. 'But all that station life changed when the unions moved in and ruined everything.'

The local put his hat emphatically on the table. 'That's exactly it! When the bloody unions interfered and made the station masters pay award wages, they buggered up everything.'

'They couldn't afford to give them jobs,' said the woman. 'They hired only at muster time.'

'That's right.' The local jerked his head obliquely in disgust. He looked out at the estuary, which was obscured by

THE RED ISLAND

the downpour; whatever he had planned to do could wait until the rain eased. 'They used to be able to kill a bullock. The wife used to let 'em help 'emselves to fresh vegies in the garden. Everyone had somewhere to live. Everyone was brought to town once a bloody month, on pay day, free of charge.'

'Yeah, yeah.'

'Then the bloody unions told 'em they had to pay 'em three hundred and fifty dollars a week, only work forty hours a week. They're not to work Saturdays or Sundays. They're only to work eight hours a day. What a load of bloody rubbish! You can't even get to where the cattle are in eight hours. And all the poor station people said, "Look, I'm sorry, I can't afford you any more." And the government said, the do-gooders who know all about it, said, "Well, that's very good. They can always go back to their lands." And every bloody Thursday night now they all get drunk and they fight the same fight they've been fighting for forty thousand bloody years. If you want to see racism, don't worry about black and white, just take a look at black and bloody black out there on a Thursday night. Then you'll see what racism is all about.'

The woman briskly sipped her coffee. Each time she put the cup down, it clinked against the saucer, its rim smeared with lipstick. 'They're intelligent at their own level,' she said, feeling the need to say something positive. 'They can't be expected to perform intellectually like us. They've got primitive minds. But as primitives they perform well. I admire them. You know, their art and their knowledge of plants. It's when they try to be like us, they start to fall apart. You give them a house and they don't know how to look after it. Not like us. For us it's natural, but they prefer sitting in the dirt than in a house.'

'But, really, the biggest problem is all the white hangers on,' the local insisted when she stopped. 'All the white scum are out there pushing their barrows. Their national parks,

east coast

their world heritage. We can thank these upwardly trendy bloody yuppies from Sydney who go to university and write books on the subject.' Suddenly he changed tack. 'Do you know where West Irian is?' he said. 'You see, most people would think it was a region of Indonesia. Has anyone had a look at the map lately to see where West Irian is? I mean, it's the other half of New Guinea.'

'New Guinea,' repeated the woman. 'Yep, that's right.'

'And where do you think the border lies? Just above the top of Cape York Peninsula. If they want to come and take over Australia, they'd come in from West Irian. It's only fifteen minutes flight, you know. But up here we've got an area the size of Victoria that's wilderness. We wouldn't even know it was happening.'

I gaped at him. 'You reckon they're going to invade, do you?'

He squinted at my interjection. 'Oh, I think eventually they will, yeah.'

The woman put her finger in the air. 'But who's up there to defend it?'

'You know I could go up there right now,' said the local, 'and take a thousand people that have never been out of the city before. And I could find them in a week and you won't find them in a year. It's so ridiculous. I think the people in the south can't comprehend how big this country is here.' He looked across the estuary again. The rain was easing. It was possible to see the white strip of beach on the far bank.

'Why do you think the Indonesians want to invade?' I asked.

'Well, this is a beautiful piece of country. If you were running out of land and you wanted to feed your nation, this is it.'

'They invaded West Irian,' said the woman's husband, speaking for the first time, although he seemed ready to slip off his seat.

85

THE RED ISLAND

'That's right, Charles,' she said, encouragingly.

'They've got it on the charts already as bloody South Irian,' the local declared.

'What, they've got Australia marked?' I said.

'They've got a piece of red that runs from Darwin down to Sydney Harbour that's called South Irian on their maps.'

'You've seen these maps?' I asked incredulously.

'A couple of my mates have.'

I laughed. 'Where?'

'As you go through customs at bloody Denpasar Airport. So they tell me,' he said leaning forward aggressively to disguise the uncertainty I detected in his voice.

'I find that difficult to believe,' I grinned.

'Well, that's a southerner for you!' He pushed back on the table and stood up. 'You find everything difficult to believe. It's happened to every other country in the world. Why do you think it can't happen to us? Jesus Christ!'

The woman sipped the last of her coffee. 'What a tricky, tricky world,' she said. The local shook his head and, unable to listen to any more of my nonsense, walked away through the rain.

———

Although the weather improved only slightly overnight, I decided not to waste another day in Cooktown. Pete was working on his bike. 'Which way are you heading, then?' he asked.

'Inland.'

'Don't miss Ayers Rock,' he said, wiping grease from his hands. 'Before I went there, I thought, yeah, yeah, what's the big deal? But when I saw it, man, it fuckin' blew my mind. You can feel the power of that place. It's awesome. I stayed for days trying to figure it out.'

'I'll keep it in mind.'

east coast

'And, I tell yer, the colours you see inland are unreal. You can't imagine it here, where it's so fuckin' green. But believe me, man, this is just the duco. Inside, she's pure red. The whole way through.'

PART TWO

inland

I DIDN'T need Pete's encouragement, but it wasn't wasted entirely. I had been travelling for two months across 3000 kilometres of territory where almost every sight was green. Now, I wanted something else. Pete's evocation of a red land fired my imagination. I booked onto a bus for Charters Towers, a town a couple of hours west of Townsville on the highway that went inland to Mount Isa and further—into the Northern Territory. Charters Towers was on the edge of the arid land that stretched over thirty degrees of the earth's surface, a vast tract within my own country that was more foreign to me than the deserts of Mexico.

I sat next to Hanna, a Swiss woman of Korean descent whose adoptive father, she confided shamefacedly, was a merchant of death. A furrier. She was a tall broad-shouldered girl with lovely tapering eyes and cheeks as prominent as her tiny nose, a trainee nurse who was so impressed with Australia that she was looking for an Australian boyfriend. She said it in such a matter-of-fact tone I knew what she actually wanted was an indefinite visa. 'A husband?' I said.

'Maybe,' she said, with a grin that narrowed her eyes.

'You must like Australia.'

THE RED ISLAND

'I do. It is good fun here. Everyone is relaxed. "No worries, mate,"' she mimicked. 'What I like most is tandem skydiving. That is the ultimate.'

'Surely you don't need to come here for that?'

'Maybe not, I don't know. But I went twice in Cairns. It cost a lot of money but I liked it too much, I went again. Next I want to skydive by myself.'

'Good for you.'

'But you are right. I can do this somewhere else. What I like is no tension. In Europe there is always tension. We have things like Chernobyl to live with. Anything like that could happen again. Who knows if what we eat is safe?'

We arrived in Charters Towers close to midnight. She was continuing non-stop to Darwin, a forty-hour trip. 'You should be careful here,' I said as we shook hands. 'It's not always safe in this country for women travelling alone.'

The manager of the hostel met the bus and drove me through dark streets to an old elevated house on the outskirts of town. I slept in an empty dormitory and in the morning shared the breakfast table with the only other guests, a soldier on leave from his base in Townsville and a young station hand waiting for his new boss to collect him. The house was restful. Its walls were louvred from ceiling to floor to facilitate the flow of air. It had lovely polished timber floors. And, because it was meagrely patronised, it retained a domestic atmosphere.

'My last bit of luxury for a while,' said the boy, who had left a job near Birdsville on the edge of the Simpson Desert for a cattle station north of Charters Towers to do a bit of mustering and fencing, to check the wells and bores, and to shift water pipes. He seemed edgy. New job nerves.

'Do you muster on horse or motorbike?' I asked.

The sides of his head were shaved, accentuating his lumpy ears and his conical skull, making his crop of ginger hair look like an ill-fitted wig. 'I prefer motorbikes,' he said, blinking nervously. 'When I get on a horse, it's a clash of the

inland

egos. Probably because both of us have got no brains.'

I looked around town. As in Cooktown and Rockhampton, old buildings from the gold rush days still stood in good repair. I passed a hall, full of hundreds of competitors in a dart tournament, and a hotel with a few stockmen leaning against its upstairs balcony, smoking cigarettes. But next to City Hall was a small park. I sat against its wall and wrote in my notebook for half an hour before I was interrupted by an Aboriginal. He asked me if I minded whether he and his friends sat in the park. 'Go ahead,' I mumbled. 'It's not my park.'

His friends, a group of bedraggled Aboriginals and a white man, weren't waiting for my permission. They had entered the park and sat under a tree near an adjacent wall. He was eager to return to them. 'You want to join us for a drink, brother?' He was tall and skinny with an angular face and fine cheekbones. His front teeth were missing. He smelt of alcohol and his curly hair was matted with dry blood.

'I'm busy, mate,' I said, holding up my notebook.

'Maybe later,' he said, giving me his hand to shake. 'Me name's Arnie. Thanks, brother.'

When I got up to leave, he called me over and introduced me to his friends. The group sat in a close circle sharing a flagon of red wine.

'Hey, I'm his sister,' said a dumpy woman. 'Where do you come from?' When I told her she shook her head irritably. 'I seen you somewhere before. You been in Townsville?'

'A few weeks ago.'

'Yeah, that's right. You were at St Vinnies,' she said.

I remembered the line of people outside the soup kitchen at Saint Vincent de Paul, just down the road from the youth hostel in Townsville. 'Near there, maybe,' I said. She seemed satisfied and offered me a drink. I declined with a lie. 'I never drink on Sundays.'

'Don't make him, don't make him!' shouted Arnie's

THE RED ISLAND

girlfriend Gwennie, whose pretty face was misshapen with a swollen eye. 'He's Christian.'

But no-one was forcing me or resented my ingratitude. The white man closed one eye and scrutinised me. 'Melbourne, eh?' His whiskered cheeks collapsed like bellows. 'You know Flemington Saleyards?'

'They don't exist any more,' I said. 'It's a housing estate now.'

'Jesus!' he exhaled. 'I worked there for bloody years.' He shook his head and took the flask.

'What are you doing up here?' I asked him.

'I've been a stockman. But I'm too crook now, mate, too crook for anything.'

Gwennie took the flask from him. 'You're not too fuckin' crook to hit yer fuckin' wife. Look at her!' she said pointing at the dumpy woman whose face looked bruised.

He scowled. 'Shut yer fuckin' face!'

I decided to go. 'You got five dollars?' Arnie asked as I stood up. 'For a pie.'

'Bullshit,' I said affably, and tossed him a two-dollar coin.

In the afternoon I went on a guided tour of the obsolete Venus Mill gold battery. The guide was a small man with a broad-brimmed hat that pressed down on his ears, a bright orange shirt, half-mast black trousers, orange socks and brown shoes. He explained the process from ore to ingot to a small gathering of tourists in straw sunhats and frocks, towelling hats and walk shorts. 'The government controlled it all,' he concluded. 'Maybe the miners broke off small bits for the black market, but most went to the government.'

'How did the government control it?' I asked. 'Who's to say the miners didn't pocket much more?'

'I guess it was a bit like cheating on tax. Some people try and get away with it.'

'They probably tried to take six per cent,' said a portly tourist with a handle-bar moustache.

inland

'Is that what you do with your tax?' I joshed, wondering how he'd arrived at such a figure.

'I don't pay taxes.' He glanced at me sharply. 'People reckon there's two things that are inevitable. Death and taxes. But if you believe that, matey, you haven't got a good enough accountant.'

I walked back into town along a dusty road. The heat stung my shoulders, the first real heat I had experienced on the trip. All the old houses of Charters Towers had high gables for insulation and gardens that mocked the climate. Yet on the outskirts of town the vegetation was withered and sparse; the ground remained yellow and cracked.

I carried my rucksack into town in the evening, intending to wait in a pub until the bus came. It was due at 11.30 p.m. I strolled towards the Court House Hotel, looking forward to a cold drink, and caught sight of Arnie and Gwennie standing outside. I remembered my declaration about Sunday drinking, and crossed the street to the bus stop. Eventually they came over, walking erratically. A near-empty bottle of port swung loosely in Arnie's hands. 'Hey, Graeme,' he said, surprising me by remembering my name. 'Can you spare five dollars, brother?' His shirt was undone and his jeans were slipping off his hips. He had no shoes. His feet were filthy.

'You've already put the bite on me today,' I complained.

'Yeah, but you're a good bloke.' They sat on the bench next to me and badgered for a while. Finally Gwennie asked if I had a spare cigarette.

'No smokes. I've given up.'

A coach pulled up and they left me to cadge cigarettes from alighting passengers. When they returned Arnie promised to stop annoying me. 'We're going to sit here with you, brother, until your bus arrives. Keep you company.'

'Thanks, but that's not necessary. I'm used to waiting hours for buses.'

THE RED ISLAND

'It's all right, brother,' he said smiling, displaying the gap where his incisors had once been. 'We don't mind, do we, Gwen?'

With her lips lingering on a cigarette, Gwennie nodded without lifting her eyes from the pavement. Her breasts dangled unevenly inside an orange singlet. Her grubby white dress came down to her shins.

'Honestly,' I pleaded. 'I don't want to waste your time.'

'We got nowhere to go tonight except home. Nothing to do there. No drink there, brother.' Arnie swigged the last of his port. 'You buy us another bottle and you can come home with us. We'll have a party.'

'I've got no change,' I said. 'Just enough for breakfast.'

'Breakfast?' Gwennie guffawed. She fiddled with a black, yellow and red headband that she had acquired since I first saw her in the park. The Aboriginal colours. Noticing me looking, she said, 'These are my colours, man.'

Behind the bus stop was a vacant lot and next to it a convenience store. Some Aboriginals pulled up in a car for petrol. Arnie and Gwennie eyed them, put their heads together, argued about tactics, then Gwennie strolled over while Arnie carefully monitored her moves. When she came back empty-handed, Arnie lifted his hand to strike her. 'You fuckin' cunt!' he shouted, but didn't carry out his threat. He turned to me. 'Sorry about swearing, brother. She fuckin' upsets me. She never does anything right. I don't know why she's my woman. Look what the bitch did to me last night.' He showed me his head where the blood had matted his hair.

Even in the dim street lighting I could see that his skull was split. 'Jesus, how did that happen?'

'She fuckin' broke a bottle over my fuckin' head!' It had happened at a cousin's birthday party. Afterwards he had grabbed a knife and held it at her throat. 'Cos that's how I go, right? Once I get like that anything could happen.' He turned to Gwennie. 'You fuckin' cunt! What ya call the

96

inland

fuckin' cops for?' Then to me. 'Sorry for swearing, brother.'

'Oh yeah, sure. I called the cops.' Gwennie was sullen, her head still drooping. 'How the fuck could I have called them, cunt? Jenny's got no phone. Did I run down the street to a phone box? They were there in no fuckin' time. How did I get down there, huh? You're so fuckin' smart, you tell me, cunt.'

Arnie gave it some thought but was distracted by an old Aboriginal woman crossing the street. 'Hey, there's Auntie Thelma,' he whispered to Gwennie. 'She's comin' from bingo.'

They swung into action as Auntie Thelma approached the store. 'Did you win?' Gwennie called out.

'Enough to buy some food, love,' Auntie Thelma replied.

A young boy bouncing a basketball accompanied her. Gwennie told me his name and said he was a good boy because he didn't smoke or drink. He showed us a medal pinned to his singlet. 'That's not yours,' Arnie muttered.

'Sure it is.' The boy laughed.

After he skipped away, a black teenage couple came along the street. Arnie rose to intercept them. The youth, who was dressed in loose pants and oversized runners, swaggered like a rap dancer. His girlfriend wore a pink skirt. They stopped and listened to Arnie, but the boy looked angry. 'I've got nothing for you,' he muttered. 'You know I don't smoke.' He pushed past Arnie, dragging his girlfriend by the hand.

Unable to stand it any longer, I fished some change out of my pocket and gave it to Arnie. It wasn't enough for a bottle of port, but it lifted his spirits. 'My breakfast money,' I said. He instructed Gwennie to wait while he went to the Court House Hotel, hoping to scrounge the remaining cost from an acquaintance who'd been there earlier.

'You should go and look after him,' I said to Gwennie. Having been anxious from the moment he'd walked away, she needed no more prompting.

THE RED ISLAND

I had five minutes of peace before I heard them screaming at each other and saw Arnie returning, with Gwennie following. When he reached the bus shelter he was empty-handed. 'That fuckin' bitch fucked everything,' he yelled. 'If she hadn't come, I would've got the fuckin' dollar. She's just fuckin' trouble for me.' Gwennie cursed him as she arrived. 'If I tell you to stay here, bitch, fuckin' stay here. Stop followin' me around.' He grabbed her and they scuffled in front of me.

Feeling responsible for their latest disagreement, I did some shouting of my own. 'Look, I don't want to stay here if you two are going to fight. I'll just go for a fucking walk!'

'She fucked my chances.'

'Why hit her?' I insisted. 'She's your best mate.'

'She's my missus,' he explained.

'And she's your best mate. You ought to treat her with a bit of respect, or she might leave you.'

Arnie looked at me wildly. 'Graeme, she never leave me, brother.' He slumped onto the bench next to me and brooded.

Gwennie sat down beside him. I felt sorry for them, and wanted to get away before I became utterly dejected. They seemed resigned to a dry night. Gwennie curled up on the bench and put her head on his lap, while Arnie stared at the road, staying only to fulfil his promise to wait until the bus arrived. When it pulled up at 11.45, fifteen minutes late, they rose, farewelled me perfunctorily, and dawdled off together away from the street light, into the darkness.

I woke in the early hours of the morning when we stopped in the small town of Hughenden for a half-hour break. I walked to the town limits away from the street lights. Without the moon or a cloud in the sky, the constellations surrounded the earth like a gauze shroud. Such a sky

inland

taunted human intelligence. A humbling sight, and I appreciated it. I knew little about astronomy. I thought I could find the Southern Cross and a constellation I used to call the Saucepan. But to attach names to this stupefying vastness seemed superfluous.

I slept soundly on the bus until we reached Cloncurry just after dawn. We stopped for an early breakfast, then headed further west, further inland towards Mount Isa. We had passed into a different world. Nuances of red earth, hills without soil, shards of rock like racks of broken crockery below a monochromatic sky.

The chimney stack of the Mount Isa lead smelter was visible over low hills half an hour before we reached the town. It was 270 metres tall and dominated the mining site, a labyrinthine complex of grimy buildings, winches, stacks, conveyors and hills of disgorged black earth, separated from the town by the dry Leichhardt River that occasionally ran north to the Gulf of Carpentaria.

The town centre was as charmless as the mine. It was on a rise from the river, a grid of wide streets with unattractive commercial buildings and scarce public space. I'd walked almost two kilometres to a hostel when a man fell over near me as he crossed the street and cracked his head on a concrete gutter. He had the wasted look of an alcoholic. His face was wan. Blood poured from his temple and his hands twitched. Although his pale eyes stared at me, he didn't respond when I spoke. Someone rang for an ambulance and, when it arrived, its officers interrogated me, as if they suspected I had caused his injuries.

After I arranged my accommodation, I went for a walk in some hills behind the town. What at a distance looked like orange soil proved to be fractured rock. It was ideal terrain for snakes and scorpions—crevices and cracks and spinifex grass. Yet the only wildlife I sighted was a rock wallaby that bounded away erratically. I moved along the ridge, stopping

THE RED ISLAND

now and then to view the low ranges on either side. It was wild arid country, which must have been forbidding to prospectors who roamed the inland long before the invention of air-conditioned four-wheel drives and two-way radios.

When I got back to town I headed for a pub to quench my thirst. I chose a saloon bar where a craggy old customer was helping a Maori barmaid rehang some pictures that had been removed prior to the town's rodeo. 'The boys go wild,' the barmaid explained. 'Although we didn't have much trouble this year.'

'That's well hung,' the old boy sniggered. He stood back to admire his work. The picture was of a busty model holding up a brand of beer. 'What I could do with her, eh?'

A couple of women sitting on a stool rolled their eyes. One was Gloria, another New Zealander, but blonde-headed and fair-skinned. She had lived in Mount Isa for eighteen years.

'What made you stay?'

'It's just so different from the coast,' she said.

'How do you cope with the isolation?'

'Everyone here gets along together. There's sixty nationalities and it's not a problem, isn't that right, Sherry?' Her drinking partner nodded. 'We've got Mexicans, Arabs, Russians here. No Eskimos, although we used to have one of them, too. No bull!' She laughed and tapped her cigarette against an ashtray. 'It's not perfect, but it's a bloody sight better than a lot of places.'

'What's not perfect about it?'

Her smile disappeared. She drew air through her nose and glanced at Sherry. 'If you want to get beaten up with baseball bats just walk around here at night.'

'Who does that?'

'The Abos.' She puffed her cigarette and tapped it again resolutely. 'An old bloke's number came up here not long ago. Won three thousand bucks, he did, and was just walk-

inland

ing home when they beat him to death. They're the only problem this town's got. They think they can take everything, ever since Mabo. They think everything's theirs now.'

'Do any of them work in the mines?'

'Oh, yeah. There's good and bad,' Gloria answered tolerantly. 'Trouble is there's too many tribes here. And the young ones don't even know which tribe they belong to. I'm telling you, they're the only ones who don't fit in here. Everyone else here gets along fine.'

Later I went to another hotel and had a similar conversation with a pink flabby man who had worked as a cook on oil rigs in Bass Strait and was now a manager of a catering firm for an exploration mining company.

'I'm getting the impression everyone in this town hates Aboriginals,' I said.

'You're not wrong. I hate 'em, although I wouldn't say that with one of 'em standing next to me,' he said, gloating about his timidity. 'Tasmania had the right idea. Shoot the bloody lot of 'em.'

It was a relief to go underground, down a mine that was the largest silver and lead mine and one of the top ten producers of copper and zinc in the world. The air was stifling and the temperature in places rose to a level of discomfort close to panic. The guide, another Maori, was amicable and witty. We dropped 850 metres in a cage, then stepped into a tunnel where we climbed into a four-wheel drive and toured some of the hundreds of kilometres of roads until we were 1500 metres beneath the surface. Much of the tour was in darkness, like a night trip down a mountain side, but occasionally we came upon a busy and brightly lit mechanical workshop or a massive remote-controlled earth mover powered by overhead electric cables. Finally the guide took us to an ore crusher that looked like a set on a James Bond movie, a huge grid through which ore fell a hundred metres to massive grinders. 'Kneel down and take a look,' he said.

THE RED ISLAND

'But don't be careless because I'm not coming after you.'

When we returned to the surface, I walked back to the hostel with a tall blonde German student from the tour group. Her name was Annika, and she agreed to accompany me to a pub that evening, where we drank German beer and discussed her studies in English literature. The bar was empty except for a rowdy group of women in tight denims and men with shaved heads and bare biceps. We were sitting some distance from them, but when I went to the bar for more beer, one of the men approached and suggested we join their little party. I declined, pretending my relationship with Annika was at a delicate stage. I wondered what Annika would have thought of the swastikas embossed on his belt buckle and tattooed on his beefy arms.

I'd expected to find racism in the outback. But I hadn't anticipated how overt it would be. Segregation, enforced by community hostility, kept Aboriginals out of certain bars and clubs. The Aboriginals here used only one pub, whose smashed windows and doors reinforced the convictions of local whites: blacks were incapable of looking after anything.

The next morning, returning from a lookout in the town, I came upon the Kalkadoon Tribal Centre. I talked to a woman there about what I'd heard. 'Pub talk,' she said. She made me a cup of tea and told me her name was Martha. 'They just like to criticise,' she said. 'I think black and white should work together. We know the mining companies and the pastoralists are not going to go away. So we want to work with them to protect our heritage.'

I looked around the centre at the artefacts and the historical accounts of the district. In 1884 the Kalkadoon had fought against the whites at Battle Hill, north-east of Mount Isa. 'We defended our land, just like Australians did in World War II,' said Martha. 'But have the whites apologised to us like the RSL demands of the Japanese?'

Finally, the morning I was leaving, I met a miner in town.

inland

He had worked at Mount Isa for twenty years. He had sunken eyes and oily skin, with blackheads around his nose. 'I expected the pubs to be full of miners,' I said.

'They mostly drink at the clubs, mate. Anyway, yer rarely see two miners in public together. They'd be tearing each other apart.'

'Why's that?'

He chuckled. 'Arguing over whether they're sharing the work evenly. A lot of the miners are on contracts these days, and they're productivity based, you see. It's important your partner pulls his weight.'

'It never used to be like that, surely?'

'We live in different times now, mate. Sometimes I work with a sheila. There're still blokes who resent the presence of women down the mines.'

'There's female miners?' I said, surprised.

'A few. If one of them's your partner, you've got to be careful none of the other miners upset her. There's a lot of abusive chauvinist miners, you know. And if they upset your partner, your work falls off. So you wait till you can get him aside, while he's having a quiet pee somewhere, and you explain to him, without words if necessary, to leave your partner alone because it's affecting your output.'

'How do you like working with women?'

'They're all right. At first I had me doubts. But, you'd be surprised at how bloody hard they can work. Harder than most of the men. They've gotta, just to prove 'emselves.'

'What about Aboriginal miners?' I ventured.

'Even bloody harder.'

———

The road from Mount Isa to Camooweal on the Northern Territory border passed through monotonous scrubby territory where meagre herds of Brahmin and Santa grazed.

THE RED ISLAND

Every few square metres the soil—red on one side of the road, black on the other—was sculpted into termite mounds. Solitary hawks shared the bleached sky with flocks of pink galahs and delicate eddies of dust. I was a thousand kilometres from the east coast, and a thousand more would pass before I reached Alice Springs in the centre of Australia—with few towns along the way.

We stopped at a Camooweal roadhouse and parked alongside several road trains. This was the first chance I'd had to inspect these articulated trucks which each pulled three penned trailers. But the heat heightened the stink of the cow shit that coated the empty trays, attracting thousands of flies and forcing me into the cafe, where drivers ate steak and eggs, and drank aromatic black coffee.

Across the border, marked only by a modest sign, the scenery changed from scrub to buffalo grass. The horizon seemed more distant. Wrecked cars and rusty forty-four gallon drums lay overturned by the highway. Passengers watched a video or made the most of the distraction to pursue love affairs. The Welshman next to me slept and the Japanese youth across the aisle solved mathematical problems. After the video the driver informed us we'd been passing through cattle stations whose average size was two million acres, and that the section of highway we were travelling went for 72 kilometres without a bend. If there'd been a bend at all since leaving Queensland, I hadn't noticed it. At one stage in the long afternoon, I fell asleep and woke to the same landscape, thinking that I'd dozed for five minutes, to find another two hours had passed.

It was dark before we reached the Stuart Highway at the Threeways junction. The Japanese lad closed his puzzle book. The coach went south for thirty kilometres to Tennant Creek and dropped off those passengers going to Alice Springs. I hung around the terminal and went for a walk along the main street. We left Tennant Creek towards mid-

inland

night. I was asleep within minutes, and when I awoke, aching from eighteen hours of travel, the coach was approaching the dark shapes of the MacDonnell Ranges.

There were certain towns and landscapes that defined my idea of Australia. One of these was Alice Springs. Its location right in the centre of the continent, at the heart of the dry land, ensured its place in the Australian psyche. It was legendary, a monument to colonial triumph, the linch-pin of a coastbound nation. I was eager to look around. When the sun rose and the shadows receded I found myself in a modern town with air-conditioned shopping plazas and a mall identical to those I'd seen from Byron Bay to Cairns. Souvenir shops along the mall sold cowboy hats and Aboriginal artefacts. Cafes offered sidewalk service. Palms and arbours offered shade. Only the surrounding MacDonnell Ranges and the dry Todd River bore any rela-tion to what I had heard about the Alice.

The ranges were low and bare. The river bed, an expanse of sand as wide as (and a good deal longer than) Bondi Beach, was used as a campsite by groups of Aboriginals. Despite the signs I saw, warning against overnight camping and the public consumption of alcohol, the river bed was littered with empty wine casks and scav-enged materials for makeshift shelters.

'It's a kind of racist law,' said Harry, an old hippie who was stranded in Alice Springs. He had a long beard and white hair which he kept in place with a woven headband. 'No drinking in public within two kilometres of a licensed premises. It was aimed to stop the Aboriginals drinking in the Todd here in the Alice, but it affected them in Pine Creek, where I was for a while. They used to like a quiet drink down by the creek then they'd wander home.'

THE RED ISLAND

The police were constantly patrolling the Todd, putting drinkers in their paddy wagons, confiscating casks. I watched one policeman from a distance as he twirled a silver bladder, emptying its contents as an old woman stood nearby.

I spent a couple of days acclimatising to the intense inland sunshine. One morning I hiked a few kilometres along the banks of the Todd to an old telegraph station and the permanent spring that gave the town its name, an old campsite of the Arrernte people, where the land was craggy and withered and quiet. In the evening I climbed Anzac Hill at the edge of town, to watch the sun strike the MacDonnell Ranges, an impressive sight that I shared with dozens of camera-toting tourists. The tourists I spoke to in town were generally unsympathetic towards Aboriginals, despite their penchant for indigenous artefacts. They looked at the Todd, and clucked in disgust, ignoring the crapulous whites in the pubs and the Aboriginals who worked in the town. I went to a football match, with blacks and whites on both teams, where supporters parked their cars around the boundary and tooted horns when goals were kicked, reminding me of games I attended when I was young. The football oval was the greenest patch of ground in town. The next day, with little reason to stay any longer, I took a coach to Uluru.

Like all Australians, I'd been exposed to the image of Uluru all my life: through photos, posters, advertisements, documentaries, movies. It would crop up somewhere, anywhere, sometimes in the most curious places, invariably under its colonial name Ayers Rock. It was on tea towels, place mats, calendars, mugs, stationery, t-shirts, sun hats, footwear, wallets, key-rings. You could buy small models of it set in a snow storm, or as landscape for toy railway sets and fish tanks. And on the east coast (where the Giant Banana, Giant Pineapple, Giant Oyster and Giant Bull could be found) I'd seen Miniature Ayers Rock, that housed an entrance to a fun park. Of course I had to see the real Uluru.

inland

After we left Alice Springs, passing through Heavitree Gap early in the morning, the land stretched between low ridges of rock. Mulga and saltbush covered the plains but the red ridges were bare and startling. I'd expected the land to be flatter; instead it looked scraped and ruffled. In the pale sky I saw flocks of black cockatoos. Most of the young foreigners on the bus were puffy-eyed and drowsy. But the Japanese boy next to me, who had showered and combed his hair, ate two boiled eggs and a lolly pop for breakfast.

We made a stop at a tourist camel farm where we had refreshments and the opportunity of a brief ride on one of its cantankerous beasts, then at a roadhouse at the junction of the Lasseter Highway to Uluru. I was eating a snack with one hand and warding off the flies with the other, when Hanna, the Korean-Swiss girl I'd travelled with a week earlier, dropped into the seat next to me. 'We are on the same bus,' she announced. 'I am down the back. You didn't see me, but I saw you.'

'How was Darwin?'

'Kakadu I loved,' she said with a neat grin. 'I saw a lot of crocodiles. Fascinating.'

'What do your parents think of you travelling alone so far away?'

'They don't like it. But I phone them every week to tell them what I've been doing, although I don't tell them everything.'

'What don't you tell them?'

She grinned. 'Look, the driver is getting ready to leave. We should move.'

Because the sealed road narrowed, it was necessary for traffic to veer onto the dirt between the bitumen and the scrub as it passed, filling the air with dust. Paddy melons grew along the roadside, introduced last century by Afghan camel drivers. After a rise, with the grandiose title of Mount Ebenezer, the scrub succumbed to red soil. For hundreds of

THE RED ISLAND

metres off the road, beer cans blown by the wind littered the bare ground. And, as I tried to spot the most distant can, I saw several crows sitting in a circle on a dead cow, peering into the cavity they had created in its abdomen.

'There it is!' the Japanese tourist declared, pointing past me at a looming shape to the south. But he'd made a common mistake. It wasn't Uluru but Mount Conner. And when the driver stopped at a lookout, the mistake was obvious: unlike Uluru, Mount Conner had a classical mesa shape. Yet I was astonished by its solitary grandeur; and more so because I'd never heard of it before. Why wasn't it on the tea towels too?

When we finally caught our first glimpse of Uluru an hour later, I understood the oversight immediately. We were travelling through dunes when it appeared beyond a sandy ridge like a harvest moon. It must have still been thirty or forty kilometres away but looked to be no more than one or two. It disappeared and re-emerged behind waves of red soil, as unsettling as a photomontage, until we reached Yulara, the resort village on the edge of the Uluru National Park, where I lost sight of it altogether. I showered and had a drink. A couple of hours later the bus returned to take us to the rock.

———

Why did I feel so fragile the moment I stood next to Uluru? I could hardly believe the emotion that threatened to overwhelm me. I was with thirty foreign tourists from the bus. What would they think if I were to voice my feelings?

'Right, this is the point yers come to tomorra mornin' if you're gonna climb the rock,' the driver shouted. 'It's closed right now because of the wind. You can get blown off just like that. Tourists don't take the dangers seriously enough. If you've got a bad ticker or respiratory problems like asthma, forget it. You're not allowed to go up. If you look at them

inland

plaques over there you'll see how many refused to listen to good advice. So tomorra mornin' I only want the fit ones comin', is that clear?' I began to walk away. 'You can go for a bit of a trot along this track. I'll meet you at the other end in thirty minutes. Then I'll take you right the way round before we go up to the sunset viewin' area. All right?'

The others started to follow me along a sandy path shaded by some spindly white gum trees. All the time beside me, this immense orange wall kept exerting its obscure influence. I was reluctant to look at it because I was afraid of how it would affect me.

'You're in a hurry,' Hanna called, trying to catch up to me. 'What do you think so far? Big, huh?'

I was grateful she'd come to distract me. 'It makes me feel rather humble,' I said without looking at her.

'Humble?' she repeated, as if she didn't understand the word. She looked up at the rock for a moment. 'Well, I will climb it tomorrow.'

'If you beat the record of twelve minutes to the top,' I said, 'they'll make you an honorary Australian.'

'Then, I'd never be able to leave,' she chuckled. 'Here, take my photo,' she said, handing me a camera as we passed beneath a small cave. She wore red lycra shorts, large runners, and a t-shirt proclaiming her sky-diving exploits. She climbed up to a section where its floor and roof almost touched, and lay on her back. 'When I hold up the roof, like this, take it.'

At the end of the walk the driver stood smoking by his bus, his skinny legs bare between navy-blue shorts and walk socks. He had a wispy moustache, thinning hair, and vertical furrows in his cheeks. 'That's a sacred site,' he said, pointing to a fenced-off area opposite. 'Women's business, so they say.'

When he began to drive us around Uluru, he turned on a microphone. 'Now if I don't tell you much about the rock as we go around, it's not because I don't want to,' he said.

THE RED ISLAND

...se we're not allowed to any more. The Aboriginals ...park these days and they tell us what we can and .. All the drivers and tour guides who come to the park ..ve gotta go to seminars run by Aboriginal elders from around here. They reckon the stories we know about the place are inaccurate.' He slowed down as we passed a section of the rock where the surface had been breached and its texture looked soft and wrinkled. 'We call that the brain,' he commented.

We passed the original motel and camping area. 'That's where that bloke went off his tree and drove his prime mover into the bar killing all them people and it's where Lindy and Michael Chamberlain camped. I suppose yers all know that story, about the dingo supposedly takin' their baby, Azaria.' The driver grinned. 'Now the Aboriginals live round here and you can't go over there. They've got a lot of money from this park since the handback. Who knows how they spend it?' He stopped the bus in a car park and led us on foot to Mutitjulu, a waterhole at the base of a dramatic fold in the rock. 'This story I am allowed to tell yer.'

The Tjukurpa, or traditional law, of Anangu—the custodians of the rock—told of a struggle between two snakes, Kaniya and Liru, at Mutitjulu. The outcome of the battle was hewn in the rock face high above us. The driver pointed to this and gave his account of the story. He led us to a small cave which was a gallery of rock paintings. 'Now I know an interesting story about these,' he said. 'But of course I'm not allowed to tell it any more. So you'll just have to make your own guess what they mean, won't yer? Don't blame me.'

We had a quick look at the waterhole. It was contained within a sandy pit against the rock, below a dark stained channel that descended hundreds of metres from the summit. 'Now, for what everyone comes to see, the sunset,' he declared, and led us back to the bus.

inland

We parked in a bay with thirty other coaches. I estimated a thousand people were there to watch the rock change colour in the fading light. Along a fenceline, Australian tourists in shorts and thongs and Akubra hats crammed together on portable seats, eating cabana and cheese biscuits, and sipping wine from plastic glasses. The imminence of accomplishing a lifetime ambition kept them cheerful. Strangers chatted like old friends. Yet, as the sun went down, the chatter subsided. The rock began its transformation. The click and whirr of cameras mimicked the arousal of nocturnal insects.

———

Later in the evening, while I was sitting at a table in the bar, Hanna joined me. 'Excuse me for the verb,' she said. 'But I am pissed.'

'Enjoy yourself today?'

'Tomorrow will be better,' she said, clumsily slipping onto the bench opposite me. 'Have you decided to climb?'

'I've decided not to.'

'Why not? You're still young enough.' She smiled unsteadily.

'If ever I had a desire to climb it, I lost it today,' I said. 'The Aboriginals who live here prefer that you don't climb it.'

She frowned at me. 'But this is a free country,' she said bluntly.

I decided to change the topic. 'Found an Australian boyfriend yet?'

'I have lots of offers of sex,' she said. 'But not of marriage.'

'That's no good. That won't get you into Australia.'

'No. So I refuse. But time is running out for me. I have only two weeks left on my visa.'

THE RED ISLAND

'Plenty of time.'

'In Darwin I met a nice boy, or I thought he was,' she said, her eyes almost closed. 'I was having coffee with him at a cafe, and then I didn't remember anything until I woke up in his room. He was ready for sex, asking me.'

'You can't remember how you got there?'

'No.' She was annoyed rather than upset. 'That sort of thing I don't tell my mother.'

I slept in while the climbers went off to conquer the rock and leave their signatures in its summit register. But I rejoined the tour for the trip to Kata Tjuta, a series of rocks named the Olgas by the white explorer Ernest Giles, thirty kilometres west of Uluru. 'Did you make it to the top?' I asked Hanna when I saw her on the coach.

'Of course,' she grinned. 'But not under twelve minutes. So I'm still looking for a boyfriend.'

We crossed a sandy plain covered in desert oaks, and stopped at a lookout for a while to view the weathered shapes of Kata Tjuta. I loved the softness of the colours in the arid landscape, which seemed at odds with the intensity of the heat and light. It was out this way beyond Kata Tjuta that the crazed fortune hunter Lasseter came and perished, sitting in a cave, betrayed by his camels which had bolted, distrusting the Aboriginals who were trying to keep him alive with damper, perhaps still believing he knew the where-abouts of the greatest gold reef in the world. But our driver preferred to tell a different tale. 'Do any of yers know the history of the Gunbarrel Highway?' he asked when we were back on the bus. 'If you keep going out this way you even-tually get to Docker River. Then you can head south and get onto the Gunbarrel, which will get you all the way right through the desert to the coast of Western Australia, pro-viding you've got the right vehicle and equipment. And do yers know who built it? Old Len Beadell. Do yers know why he built it? For a bet. That's the way things get done in this

112

inland

country, folks. He bet a mate in a pub ten thousand quid he could build a road as straight as a gun barrel right to the centre in five years. All he had was a Land Rover and an old bulldozer. He used to get four or five blowouts a day. But he did it. And do yers know what? It's only out one degree.'

He waited a moment to let the tourists ponder the achievement. 'Now, years later, when old Len was dying of cancer, his last request was to travel his beloved highway once again. He went out there, this time in a modern four-wheel drive, and he was fined and got kicked off for not having a permit. It ran across what was now Aboriginal land, you see. He died an embittered man.' The driver looked at his audience through a rear-view mirror. 'There's a moral to the story in there somewhere, eh?'

It was a pleasure to escape into Tatintjawiya, a lovely cool gorge between the highest points of Kata Tjuta. Its sheer walls narrowed to an inaccessible passage where the temperature was icy. Its silence was the sound of the eons. And our clumsy presence made no impression upon it.

———

I said farewell to Hanna and wished her luck. She was going south through Coober Pedy to Adelaide and Melbourne, then flying back to Switzerland. 'I have only two weeks more,' she said glumly.

'Not long to find a boyfriend.'

'What about you?'

'I'm going to Darwin, then down the west coast. Another two months of travel.'

'No. I mean, you want to marry me?' she grinned. 'Strictly for the purpose of citizenship.'

'I'm not the marrying type,' I said ruefully.

The next morning I returned to the national park in a shuttle bus and walked around Uluru. Except at the point

THE RED ISLAND

where tourists commence their ascent, I was alone. In three hours I passed only five other people: a jogger, whose approach I mistook for a kangaroo, two youths who were looking for a carpark, and a euphoric couple. I felt none of the unexpected emotion of my first visit. I was relaxed and content. In all the years of exposure to its image, nobody had taken the trouble to tell me how beautiful Uluru was at close quarters. The distant view of the monolith weighing down the earth was mundane compared to the perspective from its base. Its towering walls were streaked with black watermarks and pitted with deep cavities where lightning had struck. Boulders littered the ground. A harsh climate had caused the sandstone to crumble and fall away. The surface was scaly. I understood why the Anangu believed a reptile dwelt within.

For the Anangu, who kept out of sight, this was home: a mighty rock set in a desert wilderness, set upon by hordes of tourists. Of course the Anangu could travel anywhere, but before white intruders came, this was their realm. I had travelled the world, crossed three or four continents, seen deserts, jungles, glaciers, immense cities. It hardly took an effort on my part, less effort than the first whites took to travel to Uluru. The breadth of my experience of the world was vast, if somewhat thin. And it came at a price. The price was a sense of attachment and a universe of manageable proportions. I broke my hike near the eastern end of Uluru to watch a small hawk that was gliding across a concave section of the rock face, high up and barely visible. Eventually, it drifted away from the cliff, and I lost it in the pure blue of the morning sky.

When I returned to Alice Springs, I hired a small four-wheel drive car and early in the morning headed west along a narrow bitumen road through the Western MacDonnell

inland

Ranges. An hour later I reached a dusty turn-off towards some low orange hills in the south. Wallace Rockhole was twenty kilometres off the road, a neat little Aboriginal community with well-spaced concrete houses, whose green lawns cut an incongruous swathe through their withered surroundings. All the electricity poles were decorated with traditional symbols. There was a children's adventure playground. There was not a scrap of rubbish in the streets. My surprise was only surpassed by my anger. All my life I'd been led to believe that outback Aboriginals lived in shanties—a constant image of hopelessness. And here was a community which would have been the envy of the most fastidious resident of Tidy Town.

'There's no grog at Wallace Rockhole,' said Lesley, a dumpy woman whose hair the sun had bleached. 'If you're caught drinking here, you get kicked off. If you live here, to get money you've gotta do some work for the community each day.'

I was one of four people who'd arrived for a tour of the local rock art. Lesley was our guide. 'This used to be part of Hermannsburg until the handback in 1982,' she said. 'My great grandfather went onto the mission when he was eight.'

We followed her in our cars a few kilometres to the hills behind the community. 'Up here is the waterhole,' she said after we pulled up at a modern water bore. She led us on foot up a narrow winding path, showing us plants that Aboriginals used for food and medicine. It was 9 a.m., and already I was starting to feel the heat. We climbed until we reached a place like an amphitheatre whose stage was a deep permanent pool of water.

First Lesley pointed to a series of hand stencils, imitating how they were made. There were gaps in the display where slabs of the surface had disappeared. 'Taken by thieves. Maybe some white fellas, maybe some blackfellas do this.

THE RED ISLAND

Bad ones.' She then led us to another area directly above the pond where a series of concentric circles were engraved on a sloping rock. 'They're waterholes like this fella here. My people been coming here a long time.'

The main road continued on to Hermannsburg, but the bitumen ended and the surface was badly corrugated. For half an hour I bounced around in the cabin of the little car. The fillings rattled in my teeth. I saw three dusky barefoot women in cotton dresses sitting on the ground beneath some desert oaks near the side of the road, then Hermannsburg came into sight on the edge of a wide decline.

The settlement was larger than I expected. Besides the old white-washed buildings of the mission, there was a store, a petrol bowser, a police station and an estate of commission houses in worse repair than those at Wallace Rockhole. The streets and open spaces were littered with wrappings and empty plastic bottles. Aboriginal kids played football in the dust. I parked in the grounds of the mission, bought a drink at its canteen, and walked around inspecting the buildings: a simple church in the middle of a compound that was surrounded by missionary residences, servants' quarters, storehouses, school rooms, dormitories, a mortuary to cope with the epidemics that followed white settlement, a tannery, a smithy, a meathouse. Most had high gabled roofs and shady verandahs. It was only early spring but the temperature was in the high thirties.

Hermannsburg was the first Christian mission in the Northern Territory, established by German Lutherans in 1877 on land that belonged to the Western Arrernte people. Its purpose was 'to offer civilisation and citizenship to the depraved heathen through the influence of the gospel'. The son of one of its pastors, the controversial anthropologist T.G.H. Strehlow, who divulged taboo customs to the Arrernte to *Stern* magazine in Germany, had grown up on the mission amongst Arrernte children. The Strehlow house

inland

was still standing and had the musty atmosphere of a provincial museum. I could envisage young Strehlow in his knickerbockers, lace-up boots and boater, pursuing a spinning top across its polished floors, while his mother, frowning through her spectacles, taught her black maids to embroider.

In the manse on the opposite side of the compound I viewed some paintings by Albert Namatjira. The water-colourist, who had lived at Hermannsburg for much of his life, became the first Aboriginal to be granted Australian citizenship in 1957, giving him the right to vote and move freely a decade before his indigenous compatriots. The white establishment adored his serene landscapes—the mauve MacDonnell Ranges and sinuous ghost gums. Reproductions of his paintings hung in my classrooms when I was a child, and gave me my concept of inland Australia: pure, peaceful and empty.

When I left Hermannsburg, I went south along a crude track into the Finke Gorge National Park, following a river that some geologists believe is the oldest on earth. It took two hours to reach Palm Valley where the Finke River was a series of ponds and the unique red cabbage palms grew amongst slabs of pink rock. Dragonflies and wasps hovered and darted through the shimmering afternoon air; lizards by waterholes stood on their sentinel haunches; tiny fish filled the brackish ponds. This was Arrernte land, but all I encountered was contented tourists.

It was not his lucky day. The bespectacled Mormon going to Darwin had been on the coach since Adelaide. At Alice Springs I joined him. Even without a partner he looked like a Mormon; he was the only passenger in a suit. He had a huge backside but I peevishly defended my part of

THE RED ISLAND

the seat. When he started to greet me, I countered with, 'What are you doing in Australia?'

'I'm knocking on doors.'

'Salesman?'

'I'm a Mormon.'

'Come here to convert the natives, huh?' I said rather shrilly.

He emitted an apprehensive chuckle. 'I'm here doing my mission to the world.'

'Are you from Utah?'

'No. South Dakota. You know the Black Hills?'

'Sioux country.'

'That's right. They've got a reservation there,' he said, relaxing a little. 'I have some very good Sioux friends. You know the movie, *Dances with Wolves*? They were actually in that!'

As he loosened his tie, I asked him how much he knew about Australia before he came here. 'Hardly nothing,' he said. 'We had a briefing the day before we left. But Adelaide was just like home. Nice, friendly people. I hope Darwin ain't gonna be too different.'

'I have to say I don't like what missionaries do. They've damaged or destroyed just about every indigenous culture in the world.'

'Do you know the Book of Mormon?' he replied. 'It's all about the natives of America and their vision of God.'

'It is?'

'Yes, indeed!' he said fervently.

I looked out the window at the parched land, the low table-top hills. I pulled out Barry Hill's book on Uluru, *The Rock*. And seeing I was hunkering down, the Mormon opened his copy of *Ensign*.

———

118

inland

Stepping from the air-conditioned bus into the warm night at Tennant Creek, I felt as though I were arriving in a foreign land. I'd noticed it on my first brief stopover on the way to Alice Springs. Tennant Creek was the first town I'd been to in Australia where, in the streets at least, blacks outnumbered whites. They hung around outside snack bars and hotels. Families were out for an evening stroll, carrying infants on their hips, chatting to friends. I decided to stay a couple of days to get a feel for the place.

But in the small dormitory where I slept, an overworked fan made little impression upon the stench of sweat and mouse shit. The hostel kitchen was filthy. And the town in the glare of day was a miserable sight, made worse by a hot vicious wind that whipped up red dust and rattled loose sheets of iron. No one had succeeded in growing lawn like the Wallace Rockhole residents. Shops were boarded up along the highway; others had mesh over their windows. It was Thursday and the pubs were closed—a local arrangement to prevent alcoholics drinking away their pension cheques. I thought of taking a tour of a local open-cut gold mine, intrigued by a story that the two men who prospected it had only one functioning eye between them, but the weather was too unpleasant to be outside.

The next morning, I had a dip in the hostel's small pool, then spent the rest of the day drinking beer in Jackson's bar, sitting on a stool made from an old metal tractor seat. A pneumatic drill, saddles and bridles hung from rafters, and spades and steel rabbit traps were nailed to the walls as decor. A sign near the pool table warned: *No humbugging. No yelling*. The barman was an aficionado of gothic fashion: black shirt, thin black tie, tight black jeans, flowing black mane and goatee, sculpted silver rings on all fingers, studded belt. I figured the black Harley outside was his also. There was an old, incontinent Aboriginal stockman so crippled with arthritis that he was constantly creeping from his

THE RED ISLAND

stool to the urinal, a few miners in navy-blue singlets, and a couple of hefty tattooed Maoris. Next to me sat Len with white hairs growing down the bridge of his nose and out of his ears. He'd just returned to Tennant Creek after spending winter in the Victorian city of Bendigo where it was 'too bloody cold and unfriendly'.

Len had lost his driver's licence for a drink-driving offence, so his daughter had brought him back north with a caravan and set him up in a camping ground. He'd spent a lot of his life working as a truckie around Tennant Creek. He preferred life in the Territory. 'Up here everyone helps everyone. If you're down, the next bloke'll help you out. Then when you get back on your feet, you help the next poor bugger down on his luck, you see? In Victoria you can live in a place for ten years and never get to know your neighbour. There's no sense of community.'

Some Aboriginals came into the bar to play pool. Later in the evening two drunk white women—an ageing bleached blonde in a mini skirt, and a skinny, nervous, giggling girl—stumbled in and chatted to the miners. 'I've got to look after this lady,' said the blonde. 'Or I'll be in deep shit.'

'We're on a pub crawl,' the young one explained, touching her fingers to her lips to prevent a burp escaping. 'It's a hens' night. Besides, I got engaged today.'

One of the bearded miners scowled. 'Oh yeah? Where's the ring?'

'It's on this hand, isn't it?' she declared defiantly, lifting her right hand up to his nose for inspection. 'It's safer there. Besides, we don't want it spoiling my night, do we?' She began to giggle and had trouble stopping.

'Look after her for a moment, fellas,' said the blonde. 'I gotta go shake me snake.'

The miners guffawed. 'You haven't got a snake!' one of them roared. 'Well, I don't think so. It's more like a slug, isn't it?'

inland

As I left the pub, I saw a notice advertising a rodeo at Daly Waters, halfway between Tennant Creek and Darwin.

———

Bull Man provocatively called me Peter Garrett but his concentration floundered in the commotion. Ringers, stockmen, jackaroos, jillaroos and tourists pressed into the bar like cattle in a mustering yard. A female tourist distracted him. 'Hey, Dazza,' he shouted to a mate. 'Look at this. Isn't it lovely!' His immaculate white cowboy suit and white stetson shimmered against his Polynesian skin. While the tourist waited at the bar he rubbed his crutch against her buttocks.

The Daly Waters pub was a few kilometres off the highway amongst scrub and termite mounds. It wasn't much more than a ramshackle shed whose interior was lined with number plates and soiled paper money from around the world. Old gun barrels and hurricane lights hung from the rafters and walls. Waiting in the crush to be served, I read the signs above the bar: *We don't serve women here* and *Credit to women over 80 if accompanied by their mothers.* And I had time to jot down the messages on a couple of stickers: *The only true wilderness is between a greenie's ears* and *If girls are sugar and spice and everything nice, how come they taste like anchovies?*

'It's just a fuckin' joke, mate,' explained the inebriated girl beside me. A badly swollen eye made her smile seem perverse. 'I got so pissed last night, I passed out. Me mates laid me on a table. I fell off the fuckin' thing. That's how I got me black eye. They said I was spewin'. Noel thought I was dead. He said he was putting his fingers down me throat and everythin'!' She beamed proudly. 'I can't remember nothin'.'

Her name was Kerry and she worked as a teacher's assistant on a cattle station four hundred kilometres away in the Gulf country. She was thinking of entering one of the female events at the rodeo, the gymkhana, which would entitle her to

THE RED ISLAND

enter the Miss Daly Waters Rodeo competition. 'Are yer comin' to the dance tonight, mate?' she said as I reached the counter. 'Ah, come on! Yer can give me a dance!' And she gave me a lascivious pout.

Bull Man pushed in beside me and demanded a whisky. 'You'll want to root me after I win,' he called to the tourist over his shoulder. 'You're lookin' at the champ, darling! Hey, Peter Garrett, what are you doin' here?'

I walked over to the rodeo under way in a paddock adjacent to the pub. There was a makeshift grandstand along one side of the corral, but I sat on the ground in the shade of a gum tree and watched the events through a metal railing fence: poddy rides, buck jumping, calf roping, steer wrestling, bull riding. The air was full of dust and flies. A commentator announced each contestant, each result, through crackling speakers.

The atmosphere was more subdued than I'd expected. Men and women and children, dressed in checked flannel shirts, jeans and Stetsons, took the occasion to socialise. But the crowd became animated when a rider landed on his backside a couple of seconds into his event. An old man near me jumped onto a railing. 'If you can't ride that,' he yelled, 'there's no point you worrying about a bloody woman!'

One of the last beasts through the gates was a black Brahmin called Mabo. It bucked and kicked wildly but failed to dislodge its rider who was pulled triumphantly from its back by two mounted cowboys. Mabo rampaged, looking for an exit, its testicles swinging like a bell against its flanks. 'How dangerous is it?' I asked the cowboys.

They scrutinised me, wondering whether I was worth a response. A big sunburned man with perpendicular ears and yellow teeth was the first to answer: 'That depends on how bloody stupid yer are. A bloke got hurt this mornin'. They had to airlift him out.'

'What's the secret to a successful ride?'

inland

'You move yer hips,' he said earnestly. 'Don't sit cold like a woman.'

'Most important,' said another, who was fiddling with the adjustment on his chair. 'Don't have yer tongue between yer teeth.'

Another cowboy pointed to his feet and his head. 'Here and here,' he said.

'Your shoes and hat?'

'Yer spurs and brains,' he said impatiently. 'It's how far you dig those little bits of metal attached to yer boots into the guts of yer bull. Then you use yer brains to anticipate which way the bull's gonna go.'

I wandered back to the Daly Waters pub, hoping to get a lift to a motel on the highway. Bull Man was ordering another whisky. 'Didn't you compete?' I asked.

'Compete? I won! I'm the fucking champion bull rider!' he shouted. 'Where's that pretty bitch gone?' He pushed past me into a group of tourists. 'Is this your boyfriend, sweetheart? Well, he won't mind if I borrow you for a while.'

———

I was due to catch the morning bus. The roadhouse next to the motel was full of silent beefy couples eating breakfasts of bacon and eggs. Everyone seemed badly hungover. As I sat alone at a table eating toast, I noticed a cowboy at the counter. Both his eyes were swollen and black; his nose was misshapen. He seemed disorientated. The roadhouse assistant said, 'Get into a fight last night?'

'Apparently,' he muttered. 'I broke someone's jaw in two places. Had to take 'im up to Darwin. Claimed he won the bull ride.' He tried to grin. 'Let that be a lesson to the bastard.'

The bus took me along the highway to Mataranka Homestead, a resort in a pocket of rainforest, where I spent the afternoon wallowing in its warm crystalline spring.

THE RED ISLAND

Much of the countryside through which we travelled the next day had been laid bare by recent fires. The air was redolent with charred vegetation. The earth was black. But a vivid green was already appearing like a gorgeous boa around each scorched tree trunk. We reached Darwin in the evening and, for the first time since Townsville, I saw the sea.

Twenty years had passed since Cyclone Tracy flattened Darwin, but the city gleamed like it had just been rebuilt. There were still some fine old houses standing, designed to cope with a tropical climate before the invention of air-conditioning, and exceptional survivors of the monsoons. These had lovely gardens: banyan trees, with sprawling roots that formed crude cages around their trunks; bougainvillea growing against verandahs; umbrella palms that occupied dark corners. But erected on the properties surrounding them were modern concrete blocks whose doors and windows stayed closed to regulate interior temperatures. They looked sturdy enough to withstand a nuclear attack let alone another cyclone.

'It's a dynamic little city,' commented the young manager of the hostel, when I spoke to him that evening. 'Good money can be made up here if you've got what it takes.' He was a hustler who had successfully disarmed me at the bus terminal with the promise of free meals. He wore rings, bracelets, a florid silk shirt. 'It's Australia's best-positioned city for the push into Asia in the twenty-first century,' he said.

'How long have you lived here?'

'A couple of years. And I intend to stay,' he added confidently.

Annoyed with myself for having fallen for his spiel at the bus terminal, I demanded my free meal. He handed me a coupon, which entitled me to a meal at a local pub,

inland

providing I bought at least one schooner of beer. 'I thought there'd be a catch,' I said.

The pub was at the other end of town, a large dark room lined with poker machines and video games. There were a couple of pool tables in the middle of the room. At the bar, three women in mini skirts sat smoking and listening impassively to the small talk of some American sailors. In the far corner was a serving window. A young woman took my coupon and slapped a scoop of rice and stew into a bowl. 'Is that it?'

'That's it.'

'Any bread?'

She laughed mirthlessly.

I sat down to eat near a skinny man called Brian, who had a pair of crutches leaning against his table. 'You live in Darwin?' I asked.

'No, I don't,' he muttered, giving me a shifty look. 'And I wouldn't fuckin' want to. As a matter of fact, I can't wait to get out of the place. There's nothing in this town I want. What's it got to offer? Sometimes I just sit on a bus for something to do. I would've booked into St Vincent de Paul's but it's too restrictive. No grog, restricted hours.' He grimaced again and adjusted a brace on his leg below his baggy shorts. He explained he had a broken femur which was taking a long time to mend. 'It happened in Townsville.'

I gaped in surprise. 'You came here like that?' He had travelled over two thousand kilometres on a bus with a broken leg.

'Why not? What's the point of staying there?' he said peevishly. 'I got no house, no family.'

'You're not married?'

'Not any more, I'm not.'

'Did you work there?'

'Where, in Townsville? There's no work there any more. I used to be a boiler maker. I thought, ah, what's the point

THE RED ISLAND

sitting on me arse waiting for this to mend? So I come here. I wished I hadn't.'

'Do you want to go back?'

'What for? I just want to get out of here. They reckon the rainy season starts soon and it's bloody murder. I want to get out of here before then. But I can't make up me mind where to go. I was thinking of Alice Springs. Is that by the sea?'

Brian was the first of several drifters and homeless men I encountered around town. Darwin attracted them like few other cities in Australia, probably because of its warm climate, which made homelessness more tolerable, and the rumours that it was a city of opportunity. They slept on beaches, lived on the dole or badgered locals and charitable organisations for money and food. Vagabonds and itinerants had long been a part of the Darwin community. After Cyclone Tracy hit on Christmas Eve 1974, there were unofficial reports that the death toll was much greater than sixty-six. Homeless people and hippies who used to sleep on the beaches simply disappeared into the sea.

The challenge for any visitor to Darwin was to find someone who'd lived there for more than five years. Its population was young and transitory, with many people unable to endure its monsoonal climate. I met a couple of shop keepers: two years. A pilot boat operator: four years. A teacher: three months. I met some academics, picnicking by the sea, who had been in Darwin for a decade. They extolled their city's racial diversity and warned against thinking all Territorians were rednecks. The real challenge, they told me, was to find someone who'd lived in Darwin before Cyclone Tracy hit, over twenty years ago.

I went to Mindil Beach one evening, where the foreshore was a crush of people around food and handicraft stalls. Half the city's population and all its tourists seemed to be there, sampling Asian, Latin American and Middle Eastern foods, buying knick-knacks, listening to buskers. I pushed to

inland

the counter of a Thai stall and bought satay, and strolled onto the beach to eat while the sun sank into the Timor Sea. The locals were sociable, but I failed to find anyone who had been here for Christmas 1974.

Over the next few days I wandered around Darwin. I went to the museum to view its Cyclone Tracy exhibition. Photos of devastation from the air, from the ground, entire neighbourhoods flattened, streets of debris, twisted metal, snapped trees, tossed cars. Newspaper clippings, videos, radio interviews. A sound chamber that played recordings of the storm. Then, I stepped into a hall, full of boats confiscated from Indonesian fishermen and illegal Indochinese immigrants after they had crossed into Australian territorial waters. The vessels were constructed of timber, some painted brightly, some crudely hewn, a few so unseaworthy I wouldn't have tried to cross nearby Fanny Bay in them.

I visited the new parliament building—grandiose by any measure, and astonishing in a region whose population fell short of 250,000, a monument to Territorian self-confidence. I passed by the lovely old stone Government House building on the cliffs overlooking the harbour, and went to morbid Fanny Bay Gaol Museum, with its cells for lepers, and its gallows which had been idle for forty years. I went down to the harbour and onto the wharf precinct, and had coffee at a cafe in one of its refurbished warehouses. Each morning I walked around the cliffs spotting derelict campsites amongst the rocks below.

I swapped hostels, moving into the YHA in the centre of town. On the first night I was woken in the early hours by drunken athletes, in town for the Australian intervarsity games, marching along Mitchell Street chanting: 'Robinson has had his arse sucked!' Inside the hostel, the janitor shuffled down the long corridors with a broom, a sad, bony man who continually muttered: 'Come on, keep going, old boy. That's it, that's it, keep going.'

THE RED ISLAND

I hired a car to visit Litchfield National Park and Fogg Dam.

Many people prefer Litchfield to Kakadu. Only two hours south of Darwin, it is more accessible and compact; its waterfalls flow the year round; there are wonderful swimming holes; the vegetation is more varied. I spent most of the day there: observing the strange magnetic termite mounds, like headstones in a cemetery; walking through the pockets of rainforest below the waterfalls and along dusty tracks through scrub and palm groves; admiring its great sandstone escarpment. It was still September but the heat was intense. I refreshed myself at Berry Springs just out of the park, sitting for half an hour in the gurgle and gush of a small waterfall beneath a dome of melaleucas.

On the road to Fogg Dam, I stopped at a roadside hotel in a settlement called Humpty Doo, where a beer-drinking competition was regularly held. The record was held by Norm, someone's pet Brahmin bull who had skolled two litres in 57 seconds, beating the best human effort by half a minute. According to Joe, who told me the story while I ate a late lunch and drank more temperately, the bull died of alcoholic poisoning. 'And I don't reckon no bugger's gonna top him neither, not without goin' the same way.'

Joe was a temporary resident of Humpty Doo; he wanted to make that clear. Only no-hopers stayed there for good. People at Humpty Doo thought they were well off because they were able to buy cheap land and put prefabricated galvanised sheds on it. 'You get whole families living in 'em. Imagine what it's like inside one of them, mate, with the fuckin' heat we get up here.'

'Don't you go knockin' 'em,' interjected an obese woman who sat at the table next to me. 'At least we can call it our own.'

'And they think they're doin' all right,' Joe confided. His

inland

narrow whiskery chin jutted forward. His sunken eyes were bloodshot.

'Why don't they live in Darwin?' I asked.

'What for?' said the woman, beating him to an answer. She had ratty ginger hair, and like Joe was drinking beer from a bottle in a paper bag. Next to her sat a stooped old woman obsessively rubbing her swollen knuckles, until the fat woman passed her the bottle. 'You're better orf out 'ere with yer own bit of land an' no bugger tellin' yer what to do. City people don't understand it. We had Uncle George up from Perth last year. He goes to have a shower an' I hear 'im shoutin', "There's a dead pig in the bath!" So I tell him, "Well just step over 'im an' don't use soap."' She sniggered, causing her bosom to wobble like a dirigible in a gale. 'We hang the bacon in the dunny. That's the way we live up here.'

Joe ignored her. 'It costs too fuckin' much to live in Darwin,' he explained. 'It's a city for the rich. You can't afford to rent nothin'. But I prefer to stay there than 'ere, mate, that's for fuckin' sure. I've been long-grassin' it in Darwin for years. But you got to find somewhere to stay in the wet. Otherwise your balls rot. That happened to a mate of mine.'

I drove on to Fogg Dam just before sunset. The dam had been built in the fifties to supply water to a rice cultivation project that had subsequently failed. It had evolved into what I imagined was the world's biggest lily pond. I parked and walked along the road that stretched for a kilometre across the dam wall. In the auburn sky vast flocks of corellas and magpie geese screeched and trumpeted the day's end. Swamp hens, egrets and ibises were amongst clumps of reeds; Jesus birds crept over the lily pads. It was the loveliest of sights with its purples and greens and pinks, its profusion of life, its delicate flowers. The light faded quickly, stealing details, alerting my senses to the sweet warm air. I had come here to see the sunset and wasn't disappointed. High streaky clouds, harbingers of the wet season, gathered the remnants

THE RED ISLAND

of light from the sky. And, when darkness prevailed, the noise of the birds succumbed to a deafening chorus of frogs.

———

The next day I went looking for the Dinah Bar. I'd heard it might be the place to meet someone who'd survived Tracy. But the club wasn't easy to find. I set out in the dark following a narrow road around the foreshore of Frances Bay. There were leisure craft and trawlers moored at various quays, and sheds and warehouses of industries associated with the port. Street lighting was poor. I couldn't see anything remotely like a neon light or a sign to indicate a club of any sort. Eventually, I noticed a car pull up outside a yard that I'd already walked past.

A group of rowdy men got out and disappeared through an open gate. Going back, I saw a shed with a billboard advertising beer, and an open-air shelter some fifty metres from the road. I could hear the drone of conversation and see shadowy huddles of drinkers. There was a sign near the shed requesting members to register guests, but because I had arrived uninvited and alone I crossed straight to the bar.

Most of the drinkers were men in grubby work shorts and navy blue singlets. The younger men had tattoos on their arms, burgeoning pot bellies, rigid splayed legs (the beer drinkers' fulcrum) and goatees that had grown long and wiry. There were some women around, seated at crude tables or standing with the men. In the crush, I squeezed against a ruddy-faced, beardless customer in a khaki shirt, who observed me with one eye closed, then said: 'How're going, pal?'

'Not bad. A nice watering hole you've got here.'

'What's your project?' he demanded astutely.

The barman, assuming I was his guest, served me. I

inland

introduced myself to my interrogator who said his name was Gary. 'I'm just a tourist,' I said. 'Looking for some long-time residents to talk to. I was beginning to doubt they existed. But I got told if I came down here I'd find a few.'

'Well, now you've met one, pal.'

I followed him, uninvited, to a group of people who were standing around a high circular shelf attached to a shelter stanchion, and effectively joined them by adding my glass to the collection of drinks and cigarette packs it supported. 'Were you here when Cyclone Tracy hit?' I asked him.

'Not me, but there's plenty here who were,' he said, looking around. 'There's five of 'em together over there.' He pointed to one of them. 'That's Frankie. Talk to him. His story's fascinating.'

I suspected he wanted to get rid of me, but I wasn't moving. 'What do you do?' I asked.

'I'm a fisherman,' he said. I nodded encouragingly. 'I reckon I was one of the first commercial fishermen in Darwin, started out when I was a kid, just catching fish with a line off the jetties. Anything I didn't want to eat, I sold down at the wharf. I used to buy everything on lay-by. At sixteen it was the only way, but I got things. Now I've got me own fleet. And I've done all right for meself, living proof that if you work hard this country treats you kindly.'

A small man with vivid blue eyes, a shaven head, and full beard that began at the top of his ears stood next to Gary. A woman in stretch jeans leaned against his shoulder. She had short curly hair, and eyes that lit up every time he pinched her bum. 'How long have you lived here?' I asked him.

He rubbed his bald head while he scrutinised mine. 'What can I say to the second-best looking man in Darwin?' He had a heavy British accent.

'Who's the best, then?'

'Isn't it bleeding obvious?'

'It might be to you. But I can't see him.'

131

THE RED ISLAND

'I can't stand modesty in a man,' he quipped impatiently. 'What was your question again?'

'How long have you lived here, then?'

He said fifteen years. I looked at the woman, who shrugged. Gary said eighteen. 'You must all like it,' I said.

'The secret to liking Darwin is to know when to quit,' Gary said. 'I'm going next week.'

'After eighteen years?' I said sceptically.

'Yep. Everyone knows when their time's up. It's whether they act on it or not that keeps them sane.' As he closed one eye again and looked at me, I detected hostility, or suspicion in his stare.

Feeling inept, I babbled on. 'Do you think there's any truth to what I've heard, that people up here think they're different from other Australians?'

The bald man looked at the rest of the group and spread his arms in a querying gesture. 'How did he get past Pine Creek without a passport?'

Gary was more serious. 'I think we have a distinctive character here, yeah.' He paused while he took and lit a cigarette that the woman offered him. 'You've got to be a special type of person to stay.'

'What type?'

'Well, you've got to be able to endure the climate for a start. People go crazy up here during the build-up. There's a lot of violence. And you've got to be self-sufficient, you know what I mean? Not dependent on any bugger and big enough to stand up for yourself. You've got to have a healthy contempt for anything remotely official or bureaucratic which is going to interfere with your lifestyle.' He squinted again. 'And you've got to hate Mexicans. Southerners.' He chuckled but no-one else did.

After I bought a round of drinks for everyone, a small wiry fellow in shorts and thongs joined our group. It was Frankie. Another inebriated local with intense blue eyes.

inland

And the person I'd been hoping to meet in Darwin. His hair was parted on one side and kept in place with old-fashioned hair oil. He looked at me and blinked, waiting for me to explain my presence since I was the stranger. 'These people told me you lived through Cyclone Tracy,' I said. 'That must have been a terrifying experience.'

'It was, mate, it was.' His mouth distorted ambiguously. 'If I wasn't so pissed I'd tell you about it.'

'Tell me anyway.'

His eyes dulled as he began a story he had obviously told innumerable times before. He had been minding the house of a friend, who was temporarily out of the Territory, when the storm blew in. As the cyclone intensified, he had set himself up in a cupboard. 'It was the only warm place I could find.'

'Warm?' I had expected him to say 'safe'.

'It was freezing, mate.'

He'd had the presence of mind to take a candle, pen, and notebook with him. Every hour he had crept out to check the condition of the house, then returned to his refuge, lit the candle and made an entry in his notebook. He expected to die; the record was for investigators who would scour the rubble after the storm. 'What I remember most was the noise. It was an unbelievable roar, like a fuckin' great jet about to land on top of me. I've lived through some dangerous situations since then, and none of them terrified me as much as Tracy.'

'From the photos I've seen,' I said, 'Darwin looked like Hiroshima after the bomb.'

'That's exactly what I wrote in my notebook.' He frowned at the coincidence. 'In the morning after the storm eased off I left the cupboard to see what damage had been done. The roof of the house was gone, but all the other places in the neighbourhood were flattened. I thought I was one of the few people left alive in Darwin. I can remember estimating only

THE RED ISLAND

one in ten could've survived when I saw the damage. You get some idea of the power of Tracy when you see a fridge on top of a water tower, twenty metres or so off the ground.'

I asked him about the days after the cyclone. Darwin, he said, had become a party town. 'We had one big party that went on for weeks. In a way it hasn't stopped. When the bloke whose place I was staying in returned three weeks later, he said to me, "Jesus, look what you've done! I leave you in charge of me house for a few days and look what you do to it. Must've been some party." And it fucking was, mate. It fucking was!'

———

I booked onto an organised tour of Kakadu, with eight other tourists. Our guide was a gangling young man with a pitted face named Jeff who wore a khaki shirt and shorts, heavy boots and a battered Akubra. He was also our driver, cook and camp co-ordinator. He talked about life in Darwin, and said he couldn't imagine living anywhere else. He loved the Top End, enjoyed taking people to Kakadu, and spent all his spare time in the bush, hunting wild pigs and geese.

There were four athletes, three girls and a boy, on the tour. All had been unsuccessful in their heats and were taking advantage of their early elimination to tour Kakadu. The rest of the group were young foreigners—an Israeli couple and a tall Dutch woman—and George a middle-aged art student from Parramatta.

We travelled in a four-wheel drive vehicle pulling a covered trailer that contained our luggage and supplies, past Humpty Doo and Fogg Dam, through monotonous scrubland, much of it within the parameters of the Mount Bundi military training area where the tanks I'd seen the day I left Melbourne two months earlier were participating in war games with the Indonesian army. We reached the

inland

entrance to Kakadu National Park by late morning. When we crossed the South Alligator River, its banks lined with pandanus, Jeff commented: 'Some yo-yo couldn't tell the difference between an alligator and a crocodile.'

At first the park looked disappointing: a flat, dry plain covered with scrawny trees, and brown grass tall enough to limit our view of the landscape. We had lunch in a shady park beside an artificial lake at Jabiru, a town built to accommodate workers from the nearby Ranger uranium mine. We ate salads that Jeff swiftly prepared before heading north along a dusty track towards the East Alligator River and Ubirr, where the scenery changed dramatically.

The remnants of an ancient plateau rose above the plain in irregular mounds quite some distance from the Arnhem Land escarpment. The vegetation was thicker. Cork-screw palms grew next to slender white-trunked eucalypts. Overhanging folds of rock cast welcome shadows across the track. It was worthwhile, Jeff informed us, to compare the ages of the rocks around us, which were 15 billion years old, with the Himalayas, mere babes formed just 63 million years ago. All the land was ancient. And Jeff, who had spent enough of his life in Kakadu for it to seem commonplace, was still impressed by its hoary splendour.

He took us to view the Aboriginal rock paintings at Ubirr that dated back twenty thousand years. There were several galleries beneath towering sandstone shelves, which had through the millennia offered scores of delicate ochre images protection from the elements. Fine stick figures of spiritual creatures and x-ray images of people and animals covered the walls. Fifteen metres above the floor of one of the shelters were the Mimi Spirits, embodying the original transition from spirit to material world. In other places Namarrgon, the lightning man, was painted with four fingers to indicate his evil, and large gonads to symbolise his power.

'Do the Aboriginals really believe these stories?' said one

THE RED ISLAND

of the athletes, putting her hands on her hips as she arched her back a little. 'Can't they see that different groups have different stories,' she said. 'This story about the crocodile and the start of the universe, it's different from, say, the stories in Central Australia, where there might be snakes or something. I mean, it's inconsistent, isn't it?'

'That's what *they* say about us,' said Jeff, with a shadow of a smile. '"How come you believe in one god, in reincarnation, or in Moslem law?" It's a belief system. One has no less legitimacy than another.' The girl shrugged. She had expected him to agree with her. Jeff said, 'Where does the truth lie? Look, you would've heard of Coronation Hill. It's in the southern section of the park. You remember a mining company wanted to take the uranium out of it, but the federal government stopped it because the local Aboriginals objected? They say Bula lives inside, and they call that part of the park "sickness country". If Bula is released, the world will end. Now, when you think of what uranium's used for, the story rings true, don't you think?'

We climbed Ubirr, a fragment of the Arnhem Land plateau, for the view across the East Alligator River flood plain. An extended Wet had slowed its usual transformation. Most of the surface water that covered it to a depth of several metres during the monsoons had gone. But the area was vivid green from the escarpment to Van Diemen Gulf, broken only by trees beside a few enduring billabongs and water courses. While white Territorians talked of three seasons—the Dry, the Build-up, the Wet—the Aboriginals of Kakadu recognised six: Gunumeleng (the pre-monsoon Build-up); Gudjeuk (the Wet); Banggereng (the end of the Wet); Yekke (the start of the Dry); Wurrgeng (the cold weather); and Gurrung (the tail end of the Dry). It was like the Inuit having sixteen words for snow: a close association with the earth made it easier to recognise its nuances. We were in Gurrung, but the hazy land before us left an

inland

impression of late Yekke or early Wurrgeng.

The air was warm and humid, yet there was only a hint of the humidity that would make the Top End unbearable in a few months' time. My clothes were soon soaked in sweat each day, the sort of sogginess that encouraged the growth of unpleasant body fungi. I was pleased to hear Jeff's offer to take us to a resort where we could use a shower and buy some beer.

He drove for more than an hour into the centre of the park where, under his guidance, we set up tents in a dusty camping ground close the banks of the Jim Jim Billabong. The sky was full of smoke from burn-offs that at dusk became a rosy fog. As night set in, we lit a campfire, and Jeff cooked us steak, barramundi and roast potatoes. And, while we ate, he talked about life in the Top End.

'All males over the age of twenty-three shoot,' he said. 'It's changing now but hunting used to be a way of life up here. If you came to the Territory all you did was mine or hunt. We used to always have a freezer full of geese and buffalo meat. Never had to buy meat. Now it's becoming more of a sport.' All but a few herds of water buffalo on government research stations had been exterminated. They were an introduced species from south-east Asia that had done a great deal of damage to the fragile ecology of the Top End. 'Every spare weekend I still go out. All I need to take are good guns, ammo, beer.'

'The essentials,' I quipped.

He nodded ingenuously. 'Nature supplies the rest.'

'If there's no buffalo, what do you shoot?'

'Wild pigs,' the male athlete guessed.

Jeff lifted his meat with a steak knife and waved it around. 'I don't shoot wild boar, I knife them.' He was pleased with the startled response. 'I get my dogs to chase and trap them, then I kill them with one thrust, right here.' He pointed to a spot on his neck.

THE RED ISLAND

'Why?' asked the Dutch woman, frowning.

'I can't explain the excitement I feel,' he said. 'It's sort of primitive.'

'What about women?' she asked. 'Do they shoot too?'

'I don't know too many who do,' Jeff said, with a grin. 'We normally just let 'em pluck the geese and gut the pigs.'

When we finished eating we climbed back into the vehicle and went a few kilometres down the track to Gagudju Cooinda Lodge for a shower and a beer. It was a large modern resort, a strange sight in the wilderness, with all the comforts one would find in a city hotel. After I freshened up, I strolled into the bar and found George, the artist, already seated with a red wine, his gaunt head bowed in thought. 'So, what did you make of the Aboriginal art?' I prompted.

He glanced sideways at me and shook his head, as if to say it bamboozled him. I sympathised, mentioning how ignorant I was of traditional Aboriginal culture. 'It's rather shameful, since I live in this country.'

A private smile crossed his face. 'I'm smart enough to say I don't understand it either,' he said. 'There's a huge gap between our cultures, and it seems blackfellas are better at crossing it than whitefellas.'

'But theirs is an esoteric culture,' I said. 'A closed culture, with secrets and taboos. That makes it rather difficult for us to participate.'

'And ours isn't?'

'I'd say ours is more than accessible. It's thrust upon everyone whether they want it or not.'

'It still has its taboos and secrets. Look how language is used to exclude others. Lawyers and doctors, for instance. Our society isn't as open as you think.' He stared at me. His eyes were pale and watery, not an artist's eyes at all.

'So, what would you say is the main difference between their paintings and yours?'

'Theirs have a social purpose,' he said sadly. 'My only

purpose in painting, if I was to be honest with you, is personal gratification.'

Jeff woke us before dawn, and by the time a thin light was rousing the birds we were climbing into a punt with scores of other tourists for a cruise of the Yellow Water wetlands. It was the best place in Kakadu to see estuarine crocodiles in their natural habitat, to see the jabiru, a great dour stork, hunched like a judge, or rising into the air from the reedy banks like a caped magician. It was a place to see magpie geese, egrets, ibis, white-breasted sea eagles, brolgas, Burdekin ducks. In two hours we saw them all. We were even honoured by an old croc, some four metres long, casually swimming before the punt for several minutes as if she were giving us a guided tour of her territory. A boy saw another crocodile on a muddy beach, and tugged anxiously on his mother's arm. 'He might chomp them birds, mum!'

'That's life,' she said.

PART THREE

lonely road home

SOME TRAVELLERS say the highway from Katherine through the Kimberley and down the west coast of Australia is the loneliest in the world. Few towns are closer together than a couple of hundred kilometres. Between the Northern Territory border and Perth, a distance of 3500 kilometres, there is only a handful of towns, most with a population of fewer than 5000; none over 30,000. There are perhaps longer stretches between communities, like the highway from Perth across the Nullarbor Plain, but the sense of isolation is greater up north. Until a few years ago the road was not entirely sealed, which added to the difficulties of driving, discouraging all but the hardiest travellers, and leaving the Kimberley largely unseen by tourists. But now two major bus companies ran daily services along the highway and a few tourist companies operated expeditions into the region. As I left Darwin, I was buoyed by the prospect of passing through a part of Australia few of my compatriots knew much about.

I stayed a day in Katherine, which was little more than a cluster of box-shaped buildings on a hot, scrubby plain, to visit the famous Nitmiluk gorge thirty kilometres away, and to watch the Australian Rules football grand final on TV, an event that had half the nation on its backside for the

THE RED ISLAND

afternoon. I sat in a hotel with a couple of whites and several convivial Aboriginals—all of us barracking for the losing team and buying each other drinks. We were one tribe for an afternoon.

It was only the start of October but, leaving Katherine the next morning, the heat was unbearable. I was grateful for the coach's air-conditioning. Out of town, along the narrow Victoria Highway, the scrub was burnt out in places, leaving the soil exposed. Junk lay discarded by the roadside. Teasing monsoonal clouds hung over low ranges in the distance. I settled back for the five-hundred kilometre trip to Kununurra, just over the Western Australian border.

Unlike other continents I had travelled, Australia left me with the impression that the earth was sinking rather than rising; that one day the sea would wash over it until all that remained were the peaks: an archipelago. As we descended to sea level I could almost count the sediments in the exposed escarpments, the undulating gradations of colour. On the plain, dry grass grew three metres tall, and in small crevices in the rock face, palm trees grew. Ahead of us a massive black buttress loomed. It was stark and beautiful and unexpected, intriguing me as Mount Conner near Uluru had done.

We had entered Gregory National Park, and soon reached Victoria River whose green waters were so far below us it was difficult to believe the bridge was sometimes impassable in the Wet. The low hills beyond the river looked terraced but again it was a trick of nature caused by eroded sediments. The land was poorly fenced. Listless cattle huddled beneath stunted trees, their demeanour giving some idea of the burning temperature outside. When we reached Timber Creek, where we stopped for a meal break in the late afternoon, I braced myself for the heat.

Even without an ocean, the outback bore certain similarities to island nations. Communities were as isolated as

144

lonely road home

atolls. 'In the middle of bloody nowhere' was a common description of a place like Timber Creek; and that was the phrase itinerant labourers—repairing road surfaces and living in demountables near the roadhouse—used to explain their whereabouts just as a denizen of Rapa Iti might say he lived 'somewhere in the deep blue sea'. It wasn't surprising, then, that the locals displayed the traits of islanders: a nonchalant self-sufficiency, an indifference to the world beyond, a suspicion bordering on hostility towards new arrivals, and great skills of improvisation. The last was evident around the settlements: wire used to keep broken refrigerator doors shut; bath tubs placed in yards as water troughs for cattle; spare parts, plundered from old wrecks, bent and filed and honed to repair other vehicles; twine from hay bales used for makeshift belts.

At the roadhouse pub I gingerly left the bus. 'Who left the oven door open?' a passenger moaned. 'That's heat for you!' a British girl in front of me declared.

Soon after we left Timber Creek I saw my first boab tree. Its bloated grey trunk, scrawny branches and meagre foliage formed such an odd shape, I kept my eyes open for more. There were few eucalypts in sight. We travelled for a long time parallel to a distant range, until eventually the geometry changed, bringing the road and the hills close enough for me to see more boabs, growing on eroded slopes amidst the droppings of wallabies or wild goats. When finally we reached a gap in the range, we were close enough to observe how great slabs had split and fallen like stones from a neglected wall onto the barren plain.

The weather looked like breaking. Swollen clouds were so low they generated a palpable tension against the dry earth. I expected at any moment a thread of lightning to unite them. Away to the north another cloud—smoke—drifted in our direction, but I saw no flames. I was glad the wind was slight because the vegetation was tinder dry. Then, the closer

THE RED ISLAND

we got to Western Australia, the sparser the scrub became. The only signs of human life outside the coach were some caravans and machinery—what I thought were drilling rigs—left unattended in a clearing by the road. I saw thorn bushes and mulga. And the ground was as bare and hard as the highway. The hills were less angular. The threat of a storm diminished as we left the monsoonal clouds behind.

The border crossing was the first I had encountered in Australia that approximated the procedure at a national frontier. No passport was necessary, but the coach was stopped and boarded by a jovial state government inspector, looking for fresh food—a perfunctory attempt to prevent the spread of agricultural diseases. 'I suppose you'll want to confiscate my muesli,' I said.

'Oh, no, dear,' she answered. 'Nothing processed.'

My purpose in staying in the town of Kununurra was to fly over the Purnululu National Park to view the Bungle Bungle massif from the air, a flight that also crossed the Ord River irrigation scheme and the Argyle diamond mine. The town had been constructed in the sixties to service the scheme, an ambititious project to develop the north-west undertaken by the conservative government of Robert Menzies, who feared the dominoes were about to fall through south-east Asia and along the Indonesian archipelago. The west coast was our most vulnerable; it needed to be populated. The idea was to dam the Ord River to irrigate the land between Carr Boyd Range and Cambridge Gulf so that cotton could be cultivated. By the mid-seventies it had obviously become a monumental debacle, and was soon labelled Australia's biggest white elephant. In recent years, however, different crops have been introduced. And with the region experiencing something of an agricultural revival,

lonely road home

the town was full of itinerant workers, mainly foreign travellers prepared to endure a few days of extreme heat picking melons to replenish their funds.

Most of the movement in town when I arrived came from hawks propped on garbage bins in public places, squabbling over scraps like seagulls. I booked into a hostel, sharing a dormitory with some of the workers, who told me how difficult the picking was. In the evening I wanted to go for a walk around town. I had seen a reservoir on the edge of the town and wanted to take a closer look. But even after the sun had gone down, a fierce wind (strange how in the Northern Territory there had been none) dried the air and whipped up the dust, making it too unpleasant to stray outdoors. I lay sweating on my bunk, hoping the wind would be spent by morning when I was due to fly over the Bungle Bungle.

When forty or so tourists arrived for the briefing, I realised I had wanted the skies to myself, to look across the landscape beneath me without the distraction of a dozen other aircraft. Tourists who want to see the world in a pristine state are liable to unhappiness. Most soon learn the art of selective myopia in order to satisfy their expectations. I looked around the room and realised I wasn't the only disgruntled customer.

After my name was called out, I followed a young pilot and two female passengers, who carried packs, to the only four-seater Cessna in the fleet. My luck was in. Not only were we going to be the first to leave, but the women were on their way to join a hiking tour of Purnululu National Park. The pilot was going to land on a remote airstrip, which would give me a view of the Bungle Bungle massif from the ground.

I sat next to the pilot with a co-pilot's control column in front of me and rudder pedals at my feet. I thought, if he were to have a heart attack, I'd be the one who'd have to take control. As he taxied down the runway, I watched carefully what he did and tried to make sense of the panel of dials (twelve in all). I searched for the fuel gauge and was

THE RED ISLAND

relieved to see it showing full.

As soon as we were in the air, the extent of irrigation was obvious. Kununurra was surrounded by crops. Sugar cane had led the revival of the Ord River district. But from the air it was the banana plantations and the fields of melons that gave the land a neat symmetry. We flew over the small reservoir on the outskirts of town, the market garden area known as Packsaddle Plain, and followed the Ord River valley upstream for fifty kilometres till we were over the dam, travelling at 120 knots and a height of 1500 feet. From the sky, the concrete wall looked insignificant, but it could retain a flood-level capacity of 34 billion cubic metres. 'Lake Argyle,' the pilot shouted, 'is nine times the size of Sydney Harbour.' Yet it wasn't this size that impressed me. The crops were finally out of sight, and before us lay the expanse of water, whose colour was silver in the distance but black below us, set in a vast barren landscape. The first glance was like discovering a lake on the moon.

It seemed remarkable that so much fresh water could collect in an arid wilderness, the outcome of a single engineering feat. It reminded me of the unhinged beauty of surrealist paintings, of a landscape mocking nature. Not much vegetation grew along the shore; but then the visible land was merely the tops of denuded hills, the soil having disappeared long ago. I was so engrossed in the view that my anxiety about flying subsided.

The pilot was pointing out features on the ground and shouting facts at us. He was looking around the sky as well, checking the location of the rest of the squadron. I followed his gaze and saw two planes no bigger than birds on the starboard side. We flew along one side of the lake, next to the Carr Boyd Range.

After we had crossed the upper reaches of the lake, the pilot pointed to the Bow River diamond mine that worked an alluvial deposit, an ancient lava flow. Its source was an

lonely road home

extinct volcano near the Argyle diamond mine, which we could see in the distance. Between the two was a dry river of diamonds. There was an airstrip servicing Argyle, and pilots who had landed there told stories of glittering stones beside the entire length of the runway.

We flew across some open territory and then some parallel ranges whose narrow ridges looked like carefully made stone walls. Verdigris spoiled the lustre of the copper-coloured land, a green tinge of vegetation that extended to a craggy plateau on the horizon. What surprised me as we flew across the ranges was the amount of water lying in depressions and channels. The land was parched, but the distance between drinks wasn't life-threatening.

The craggy plateau crumbled to pieces as we approached. The Bungle Bungle was an ancient massif, a series of conical peaks rather than a solid platform of earth. There was something grotesque about it, as if it had features in common with acne or psoriasis, an unhealthy eruption on the surface. But if this was geologically misleading—for water had shaped these ancient sediments—it was also a distortion attributable to our unique perspective from the sky, where the land around seemed as smooth as skin. It wasn't until we were closer that I noticed the unique striped surface, the black and orange layers.

I went silly with my camera, hoping to capture the images I saw through the Cessna's grimy windows. The pilot assisted by banking the plane and flying low until Livistonia palms growing in chasms seemed just beyond the wing. It was noisy and stifling in the cabin. I felt nauseous. I half-expected to vomit. But I kept snapping, for it was an experience I was afraid I would never repeat. Then we flew beyond the massif, arching around, heading for a dirt strip on the plain.

THE RED ISLAND

We survived the bush landing and, despite the trouble the pilot had restarting the engine, we flew safely back to Kununurra with replacement passengers. Now that I was back on ground for the rest of my trip, and my stomach had regained some equilibrium, I was eager to set out for Fitzroy Crossing, where I hoped to join a tour into the Kimberley. The bus wasn't due to leave until the evening, so I hiked to Hidden Valley National Park just outside of town. It was only a couple of kilometres, but the heat was intense. I soon drank my container of water and found myself dodging between meagre bushes. High above, circling in the sky, were the silent Kununurra hawks. The evening before they had seemed harmless. But here, in the middle of a searing gorge, their presence was rather menacing. The heat I was feeling was from their kitchen.

As I reached the heart of the park, I saw a stationary campervan and two people standing nearby, studying a noticeboard. 'I'm Jack Crawford and this is Brenda, me better half,' said a stocky man with a healthy sheen and bandy legs. His wife was suntanned and attractively plump. He asked me where I came from. 'Well, I'll be buggered! So are we. What part?'

They lived in Balwyn, a middle-class eastern suburb of Melbourne, and were taking an eighteen-month trip around Australia in the opposite direction to me. 'Jack's just retired,' Brenda said. 'This is our first time around.'

'We've been wanting to do it for years,' Jack drawled. 'Never had the chance before this.' They had come to Wyndham from Derby along the Gibb River road. 'The Kimberley's just bloody beautiful. I don't know, mate, we don't know how lucky we are to live in a country like this.'

'It's God's own,' said Brenda.

We talked for a while. They were decent people, the sort of Australians who had worked hard all their lives, bought their own home, raised a family, ensured their children had

lonely road home

a good education, watched them grow up and get married and begin their own families. And now it was time to relax and enjoy the twilight years together. It was their reward for an honest life. They had chosen to travel around Australia. Like many retired couples—I had noticed them all across the country—they were making what seemed like a pilgrimage. They would visit every corner of the land they called their own, at their own pace and off their own steam. And, like pilgrims, every day was a marvel; every day had new wonders. I admired them, applauded their good sense and aplomb. They had discovered the pleasure of travel late in life but were approaching it with no less enthusiasm than I had in my youth.

When I returned to Kununurra, I sat for an hour in its shopping plaza, appreciating its frosty air-conditioning and the cafe that sold cold drinks. In the evening, I collected my luggage and caught a coach for Fitzroy Crossing.

When we stopped for a meal break at Turkey Creek Roadhouse around 8 p.m., I sat next to a dumpy Aboriginal woman whose head was heavily bandaged. I asked her what had happened. While she spoke she waved her hands around and pulled her dress above her knees as if she were suffering in the heat. She told me she had been in a car that hit a truck. A teenage boy with her had been killed. She had injured her head when she was thrown from the car. The boy's death was distressing her. When I asked her where she lived, she answered, 'In the community.' I pressed her to be more specific. 'Over Bungle Bungle way,' she said. Then the coach driver called on his passengers to board.

Some time in the night we passed Halls Creek, on the edge of the Great Sandy Desert. Even in the darkness it looked ugly and hot. We stopped for a moment at a store and were on our way, along the southern edge of the Kimberley. It was 1.30 a.m. when the bus pulled into Fitzroy Crossing. I stepped into warm air, blinking from sleep. After

THE RED ISLAND

the driver removed my pack from the luggage compartment, an old bloke who looked like W.C. Fields in a wide-brim hat picked it up, and threw it into the back of his four-wheel drive. He was from the hostel at the town's original site, several kilometres away.

'The bus was on time!' he roared, pulling at his craggy nose, as we headed into the darkness. 'That's a turn-up.' He seemed to be bursting with indignation. 'Things running on time around here. What next?'

'Something unusual about that, is there?' I murmured.

'Too bloody right there is!'

I wondered which way he preferred it. 'Never mind,' I said, battling to keep my eyes open. And, winning the battle, I saw the shapes of two people on the road ahead. The headlights caught the white in their clothes.

The driver pulled alongside them, and ordered me to wind down the passenger window. 'What are you doing, Lucy?' he shouted. 'Out at this bloody time of night. Come on, get in girl, I'll give yer a lift to the turn-orf.'

Lucy and her male companion were Aboriginals. They jumped in the back, and we drove in silence until the junction. 'Thanks, Mr Rogers,' Lucy said softly as they got out. The driver said nothing.

The hostel was an old cement sheet and timber building on stilts. I crept into a dormitory of sleeping men. Its overhead fans were whirling at top speed and the walls of louvred windows were wide open. When I woke in the morning, most of the men were gone. I went to sign in. The receptionist, a wiry middle-aged woman, read my registration details. 'A Melbourne boy,' she commented.

Her name was Dot and she came from Brighton, a Melbourne suburb on Port Phillip Bay. 'Why did you come up here?' I asked, intrigued by people who left suburban life for somewhere remote and harsh.

'I'd had enough of being a psychiatric nurse.' Now she

lonely road home

worked for the hostel, which was owned by the Bunuba Aboriginal community. She noticed my interest and said, 'They're getting into ecotourism, too.'

'And the old bloke who picked me up last night,' I asked, 'does he work for the Bunuba?'

'That's Ernie Rogers. You could say that, yeah.' Then to assist her employer, she said, 'There's tours to Windjana Gorge and Tunnel Creek, if you're interested.' Since this was my main reason for stopping here, I booked onto the tour for the following day, then asked about visiting Geikie Gorge, ten kilometres down the road. 'There's tours there, too,' she said. 'But you'll have to hitchhike. The backpackers' mini bus is broken down or we could've run you out there.'

After my experience, hiking two kilometres to Hidden Valley, I decided to have a rest day. I stepped outside to look around. The hostel had once been the Fitzroy Crossing Post Office. It had a shady verandah along the front and a broken windmill at the rear. There were worksheds around a yard for vehicles, space on a lawn for travellers' tents, and further back an area fenced off with wire netting that might once have been a vegetable garden or a chicken run, but was now overgrown with withered weeds. Adjacent sheds in ruins gave the impression of an abandoned project. At the side of the hostel I found an old rotary clothes line, still in working order, and I stood for a while pondering its history. It was a long way from Brisbane.

I strolled away from the buildings until I reached the Fitzroy River. It was a hundred metres wide and contained fresh water sharks, stingrays and sawfish as well as crocodiles, but the water level at this time of year was low enough—trickling across an extensive stony bed—for me to feel safe about removing my shoes and cooling myself in the shallows. I tried to imagine what this tranquil scene looked like in the monsoon season when the river rose more than

153

THE RED ISLAND

fifteen metres. For years, until a new bridge had been built where the current town stood, annual floods had frustrated all transit of the Kimberley.

In the afternoon I stayed inside the airy hostel, reading Howard Pedersen and Banjo Woorunmurra's *Jandamarra and the Bunuba Resistance*, an account of indigenous people's attempts to prevent the white invasion of their land in the 1890s. The defence was led by an enigmatic Aboriginal, Jandamarra (whom the whites called 'Pigeon'), whose unconventional military strategies confounded and ultimately unnerved the white intruders. Jandamarra's fortress and sanctuary was the cavernous Napier Range. His favourite place of ambush, and the only pass through the range to his people's territory, was Windjana Gorge.

I was eager to visit the area. When I set out the next morning in a luxury all-terrain vehicle with Joe, our driver and guide, Julia, his girlfriend, and three other tourists, I had a heightened sense of expectation. Joe was a robust man with a gaunt sunburnt face and cropped black beard, dressed sensibly in a long-sleeved shirt and trousers. He had worked in the Kimberley for years. We headed west along the highway, travelling through the sort of scrub I had been seeing through bus windows for weeks. I asked him why the Aboriginal community employed whites to run its tourist operations.

'The Aboriginal people who own the business are very shy,' he said. 'You've got to realise a lot of the people in these parts have had little contact with whites. Many of them don't speak English. If they do, it's often Kriol. Maybe when their businesses are well established and they feel more confident dealing with tourists they'll play a more visible role.'

We turned off the highway after almost an hour and headed north through savannah country, across Black Soil Plain towards the Oscar Ranges, which from a distance reminded me of a row of rotten teeth—stunted black craggy

154

lonely road home

outcrops that looked rather menacing. They rose abruptly from the plain like some form of sinister intrusion. The other tourists, all Britons, were quiet as we passed.

There were boabs growing at the base of the range, urn-shaped and grey, without leaves. 'Aboriginals have a story about how the boab grew into a huge tree and became arrogant,' Julia remarked. 'So one of the Dreamtime creatures uprooted and replanted it upside down.'

'In Africa the same tree is called the baobab,' Joe added. 'And the same kinds of story exist there amongst the native Africans.'

There were more rocky ridges, the Napier Range, which we passed through at Cherry Tree Gap. The track ran along its western flank across Fairfield pastoral lease, which had recently been returned to the Bunuba people. We stopped for a while to view a frill-necked lizard, inert and alert on the hot powdery track, and again at the ruins of Lillimooloora, an old settler's homestead built close to one of the perma-nent springs that gushed from the range's black cliffs. In the early 1890s it had been used as a jail, but all that remained for us to see were crumbling stone walls. It was here that Jandamarra, a tribal outcast, a crack shot and a gifted horse-man, employed by the police as a black tracker in the unorthodox role of pursuing members of his own tribe, shot a white policeman and released some Bunuba captives, sig-nalling the start of a guerrilla resistance that was to last for several years.

Windjana Gorge, a short distance away, was the key to the pastoralists' expansion. Beyond it lay the rich land of the Kimberley. It was this strategic passage that Jandamarra chose to defend and, a few days after the death of the police-man, he and a group of Bunuba ambushed four stockmen herding cattle to waterholes in the gorge.

I couldn't look at its entrance without imagining the drama that had unfolded here. The range towered above us

THE RED ISLAND

like a grim cathedral. It seemed haunted. Its colour was morbid: red ochre half-draped in a black layer that had the appearance of melted icing. As we walked into the gorge along the dry bed of the Lennard River, I suffered a sense of intrusion. We approached the first waterhole, a long slender pool around a boulder, and the silence was shattered by scores of corellas that burst into flight, out of eucalypts at the base of the gorge, and raucously protested their way to the other side.

'They're permanent residents here,' Joe explained, laughing at our jumpiness. 'And that's Jandamarra's Rock.' Small crocodiles lazed in the shallows, suggesting that the river never dried completely; they swam off behind the boulder as we approached. High above in the limestone cliffs were caves from which Jandamarra and his band had fired upon the stockmen.

'The whole range is limestone dating to the Devonian age,' Joe said. 'The Napier Range and the Oscar Range were once part of a coral reef, similar to the Great Barrier Reef off the coast of Queensland. The black colour is lichen that grows in the porous surface. The range is a series of caves and tunnels, and the surface on top is incredibly rough and as sharp as knives.'

The black lichen lent Windjana its gothic eeriness. The caves and the treacherous surface had denied the troopers and an assortment of hopeful assassins the opportunity to corner Jandamarra. Their footwear was cut to pieces in pursuit of the barefooted Bunuba, who would disappear into holes in the ground to re-emerge safely kilometres away.

Despite the crocodiles we went for a swim—after Joe's assurance that they wouldn't attack us. When I was up to my neck in the water and he was grinning from the bank, it suddenly occurred to me that he had a host of tourists hidden along the ridge above, waiting to observe croc feeding time. We survived, returned to the vehicle, and backtracked to

156

lonely road home

Tunnel Creek, a subterranean stream running through the Napier Range. It was possible to walk into it one side and a half hour or so later emerge at the other. Equipped with powerful torches we set out.

The moment we entered, through a gaping hole surrounded by pink marbled sandstone boulders, the temperature dropped. It was lovely and cool and dark. Gingerly we followed Joe and Julia, stepping along a ledge beside the water. There were flying foxes and tiny bats clinging to roots that crisscrossed the ceiling. Stalactites dripped water. In places we waded up to our knees across the stream to find a path against the opposite wall. Then a vague light filled the tunnel, enough for us to turn our torches off. The light intensified as we approached a place halfway through, where the roof had caved in. Roots reaching down from the trees above hung like a frayed stage curtain along the breach. In the second section of the tunnel we had to wade across a pool up to our chests in icy water. Halfway through, Joe told us it was occupied by a crocodile. (And on our return, before I climbed in the pool, my torch lit up two red eyes in the water.) We climbed into a claustrophobic cave at the side of the tunnel to view some stalactites, then traipsed through shallows to the south side of the range, emerging into sunshine at an idyllic secluded gorge. This part of the range had been a favourite hideaway of Jandamarra in the years when he was successfully eluding his hunters.

He had stopped shooting whites when his enemies retaliated by killing innocent Bunuba. Instead, he chose to harass them, breaking into their barracks at night to steal food and equipment. He would taunt them from the ridges, and disappear into caves when they pursued him. And, returning to their bases, they would find the 'Pigeon' had raided their store. His escapes, his daring and the arsenal of weapons he had stolen intimidated the settlers enough to discourage further attempts to drive cattle through Windjana for the next

THE RED ISLAND

few years. The stand-off might have continued indefinitely, but on one of his forays to free some Bunuba prisoners Jandamarra was wounded, and another black tracker with a formidable reputation eventually found him, following a trail of blood to Tunnel Creek. The tracker hid behind a boab tree and fired at Jandamarra, who was standing on a pillar near the entrance to the tunnel. Jandamarra failed to take cover, was shot again, and fell thirty metres to his death. The creek where he had fallen was crystalline. Overhanging trees filtered the harsh sunlight, and leaves floated on the quiet water. 'Let's have another swim,' one of the Britons suggested.

———

Half the guests at the hostel were tourists; the rest worked in the district on agricultural and mining projects, or were looking for work. People talked about the 26th parallel as if it were an industrial determination. Anywhere to its north guaranteed hardship money for working so far from civilisation. Some sort of inducement was necessary to lure people into such a hostile climate.

I was hoping to get a lift into town with Julia, who had the morning off to go shopping. 'There's a coffee shop in town I keep profitable,' she grinned. 'We can have a proper cappuccino.'

At the last minute Greg, a Canadian, who had just finished working for a seismological company in the Great Sandy Desert, joined us, carrying a didgeridoo. Its resin mouthpiece had come loose, so he was taking it to be fixed by the man who had sold it to him.

Fitzroy Crossing was much smaller than Kununurra. There was a modern, air-conditioned supermarket and a row of small shops, staffed mainly by whites but dependent on business generated by the Aboriginal community. While

lonely road home

Julia went shopping for groceries, Greg found his didgeridoo vendor outside a small art gallery at the end of the row. The stout grey-bearded Aboriginal was sitting cross-legged on the ground, where he made a tiny fire from scraps of paper and twigs to heat the resin until it was malleable. I waited outside the supermarket at a bench table. Opposite me sat an old Aboriginal woman, tormented by children who grabbed her beanie and threw it away, pulled at her hair, and abused her, until an old man threatened them with a stick.

I caught up with Julia in the cafe, which was really a fast-food joint specialising in monster beef burgers. But its staff made a palatable cappuccino. When Julia arrived she joked with the youth behind the counter before she joined me. I liked her openness with people and the way she laughed, honestly and without restraint. She had a lovely full face that radiated happiness. Sitting down, she inquired about my drink. 'They're nice people,' she told me. 'And I couldn't live here without their coffee machine.'

'What do you do up here?' I asked.

'I ask people about their dogs.' She laughed at my mystified frown. 'I'm doing research into the relationship Aboriginals have with their dogs. It's part of a health project, the idea being that by getting rid of parasites in the dogs, the incidence of infestation in the Aboriginal community will decline.' She told me that older people have about ten dogs each; young people prefer two. Their dogs were considered friends, goanna hunters and guards. And they often slept with them at their sides, exacerbating the health problem. 'Since many of the Bunuba don't speak English, I show them pictures representing different attitudes ranging from kindness to cruelty. In relation to dogs they invariably point to kindness.'

I had often heard that Aboriginals had a special bond with dogs, yet so far on my trip I hadn't seen it. Not in northern

159

THE RED ISLAND

Queensland or in Central Australia; in Tennant Creek and Katherine, both with large Aboriginal populations, I couldn't recall seeing more than a few strays. I hadn't seen any in Fitzroy Crossing. 'I can understand the dog thing,' I said. 'But what's more intriguing is that after two hundred years of contact there are still Aboriginals who don't speak English.'

Julia finished her coffee. 'Let's go over to the Karrayili Centre,' she said. 'You might find that interesting.'

The Karrayili Adult Education Centre was set up in 1981 to improve Aboriginals' literacy and numeracy skills. *Karrayili* was a Walmajarri word that meant 'middle-aged people'. But the centre soon broadened its definition and its scope. 'The philosophy of Karrayili Adult Education Centre is based on that of empowerment,' I read in its prospectus. In the mid-eighties entrepreneurs tried to use staff at the centre as agents to purchase Aboriginal art, which was beginning to set new sales records in the southern capitals and overseas. 'Everyone wised up,' said Karen, the staff member showing me around. 'The artists decided not to sell any, but to have their own exhibition instead. So they needed skills in English to survive in the big cities, like purchasing a tram ticket or getting a hotel room, and dealing with the cultural differences.'

At dusk, back at the hostel, I found Greg in the yard beneath the open bonnet of his car. 'What's wrong with it?'

He stood up and wiped his hands on a rag. He had a rather delicate sculpted face, with sunken temples and his short fringe stood up at the front in scholarly style—like someone accustomed to reading with his hand supporting his forehead. It made him look intelligent. 'Nothing much,' he said. 'I'm just cleaning the spark plugs and distributor, and brushing off the sand. If I treat her fine she gives me no problems.' He lowered the bonnet and pressed it shut. 'Want to come to the pub? I promised to buy a beer for Eddie, the guy who fixed my didgeridoo. He's an artist.'

160

lonely road home

The Fitzroy Crossing Inn was halfway to the highway, neither in the old town or the new. At the rear of the hotel was an open-air bar that might have, in daylight, afforded a good view of the river.

Eddie was in the bar, waiting. After Greg introduced us and bought a round of beers, he excused himself. He had spotted two of the seismologists he had worked with, and went to have a chat. I stayed beside Eddie, and talked about his art. He was a quiet man. When he was not sipping beer, he clasped his hands together and rested them on his thick thighs. He observed me with dark eyes concealed beneath a heavy brow, and responded laconically to my questions. When I asked him what he painted, he answered, 'The old stories.' He had been to Melbourne the previous year with an exhibition of his works. 'Big place,' he said. I asked him if his people were Bunuba. 'Gooniyandi,' he said. 'Not many speak this now.' (About a hundred, I discovered later.) I talked about Windjana Gorge. He shook his head. 'Old people finished now,' he said.

I asked him a few questions about his life. He had worked on Fossil Downs Station, and was there during World War II. 'We walk them cattle to Broome, and then them bombs come. They fall. Falling on all them cows. Cows run everywhere.'

It was the first I'd heard of Japanese wartime raids on Broome. 'What about you?' I said. 'Were they falling on you?'

'Yeah, us fellas, too.'

'You still work at Fossil Downs?'

He shook his head. 'Pension now.'

Eddie was momentarily distracted by a woman in a grubby white t-shirt, who whispered something in his ear, then sauntered away laughing shrilly. He sat with his head bowed, thinking. 'She loose woman, that woman.'

THE RED ISLAND

I was about to buy us more beer, when a young woman in a mauve dress arrived at my side. Eddie said, 'You gotta buy one more, for her. She's part of my family.' Her name was Jenny. She was tall and skinny, almost emaciated, but had a pretty face despite the absence of her front teeth. I smiled at her and ordered an extra beer.

When I told her my name, she shook her head and corrected me. 'Goonangdji.' I felt flattered that she wanted to rename me with a Gooniyandi word. She talked to me while Eddie chatted to another white man. 'My husband, he dead,' she said. 'Blackfellas kill him.' She indicated the race of the murderers by pinching her own flesh. 'And my children gone.' She spoke in a despondent murmur. She had three children. Two were with her grandmother in the bush, while the third was somewhere in Perth. Her shoulders drooped, her elbows pressed against her side, and she fidgeted with her hands.

Another woman, her cousin, arrived and cheered her with a playful embrace. The cousin, Sandra, who had short cropped hair and huge soft lips, grossly overplayed a seductive look to cajole a beer from me. I laughed and yielded, buying Jenny and Eddie another as well. The white man with Eddie tried to join us, hoping my generosity might extend to him, but Jenny loudly abused him.

'Why's he an arsehole?' I asked her, watching him retreat to a table where several young men were seated.

'That white cunt likes to fuck black women,' she explained. She took a cigarette Sandra offered her, lit up, and had a coughing fit.

I told Sandra my name and she immediately called me Goonangdji. 'How did you know?' I asked.

'You've got a dead fella's name. Can't use your name. A blackfella died with your name. So you're Goonangdji.' Somewhere in Fitzroy Crossing, an Aboriginal called Graeme had recently died, making my name taboo.

lonely road home

Goonangdji was a generic term, a substitute.

I asked them about their schooling, and Jenny said she had been to a reformatory. She had been arrested as a child for drunkenness and sent away. 'We used to climb them trees to get away from the police. Now there's a sober-up room in Fitzroy Crossing where you can go for a sleep.'

We chatted for a while, then she asked for another beer. Sandra was talking to Eddie. I said to Jenny, 'It's your shout. Where I come from, if I buy the first beer, you buy the next one. I've already bought two rounds, and I'm not getting another until you get one.'

She hunched glumly. 'But this is Fitzroy Crossing.'

While we had been talking the pub had become quite busy. There were a lot of Aboriginals, not all of them down-and-out like Jenny. I noticed two tall black girls in designer clothes, with gelled hair-styles and subtle make-up. I saw an Aboriginal man in a suit, his tie hanging loose like an overworked lawyer. There were more whites than blacks, from a range of social backgrounds it seemed, the majority of them with the demeanour of alcoholics.

Two policemen arrived. They sauntered through the bar, and as one of them came our way, Jenny called to him: 'Holmes!' I noticed his wry smile, but he didn't answer her.

'Is that his name?' I asked.

She sniggered. 'John Holmes? You know him?'

'No.'

'The movie star. You know him? Blue movies.'

'I've heard of him.' Or more to the point, I'd heard about the length of his penis.

The policeman came over. He ignored me, but had a joke with Jenny and Sandra. She called him Holmes again, and he grinned and went away.

'They okay with you?' I asked.

'Yeah,' she said. 'You going to get me another beer?'

Greg arrived with his seismologist friends. 'Has Eddie

THE RED ISLAND

talked you into buying one of his paintings yet?' he asked me. 'They're in the gallery in town.'

'I'd like to see them. But I'm leaving tonight,' I said, genuinely disappointed.

When everyone had gone to bed at the hostel, I sat up alone, waiting for Ernie Rogers to come and take me to the bus terminal. I was catching the coach at the same time as I had arrived, at 1.30 a.m. By 1.20, with no sign of him, I began to panic. By 1.25 I saw car lights approaching. Ernie got out of his wagon and threw my luggage in the back.

'Bus running on time is it?' I asked him, to kick off the conversation. His eyes were red. He rubbed his craggy nose.

'Your guess is as good as mine.'

Travelling slowly along the dark road into town, I said, 'Sorry to keep you up late.'

He wiped his hand across his face. 'I've been up since four this mornin',' he yawned. 'Had to go to Broome to pick up a couple of bodies.' I stared at him. 'Another one in Derby. I shoved them in the back there.'

I looked around. No bodies. No coffins. Only my ruck-sack. 'What are you, the undertaker, or something?' I said uneasily.

'Amongst other things.'

Every hostel in Broome was full except for the Last Resort, which advertised its evening's entertainment as 'Bonfire, Music, Surf & Sex'. I had spent the night on the bus, passed through Derby on the coast before dawn, and arrived in Broome in time for breakfast. Broome had become known on the backpackers' circuit as a 'party town'. I had read about its pearling industry, its Japanese divers, its oriental atmosphere, its turquoise sea. I was expecting a shanty port. Instead, like Alice Springs, I found a bland town

lonely road home

preparing for a tourist boom. Even Chinatown, the old quarter, had been spruced up. My guidebook warned, 'Some of the plain and simple wooden buildings that line Carnarvon St still house Chinese merchants, but most are now restaurants and tourist shops.' I made an excursion into the area to see its famous outdoor cinema, located in a corrugated iron compound, now disguised by the sort of decor found in art house cinemas all over the world. Then I walked down to the shore.

Roebuck Bay was lovely. Its sandhills were red, and the sea was exactly the colour I had hoped. A buffer of mangroves extended into the translucent shallows. Offshore was a tiny island, with some kind of structure built on it, and further out a low black strip of reef. It was the first time I had laid eyes on the Indian Ocean (except from 35,000 feet above) and I was as impressed as when I had first seen the Caribbean. I walked down to Streeters jetty at the start of a channel cut through the mangroves, where pearling luggers used to unload before plastic buttons in the fifties all but destroyed the mother-of-pearl industry. With the tide out, the old timber structure looked obsolete and neglected, as if the sea along with the pearlers had deserted it. There were some derelicts drinking flagon wine on the wasteland behind the mangroves.

'The problem with Broome,' said a middle-aged barmaid at a pub I found away from the tourist precinct, 'is that too many people wanted to become millionaires in one year instead of five.' An air strike and a financial crash, which ruined many high-flying Western Australian entrepreneurs in the late eighties, had brought a halt to a lot of the development around Broome. 'So it could be more touristy,' she said wryly.

At this pub, which was hosting a darts tournament in its large bar, I met Sonny, an ex-pearler of Malay and Aboriginal descent. His wavy dark hair was oiled back like

165

THE RED ISLAND

an old-time rocker. He had so many scars around his eyes that he had no eyebrows left. Sonny told me he had been a boxer. He had fought as a bantamweight in Japan and New Mexico. But it was his pearling experience that I was interested in. 'Put it this way,' he said answering one of my questions, scratching a sallow cheek thoughtfully. 'When you go pearling, you're signing your death warrant. My daddy went pearling. He went out there and never came back. No funeral for him. When you're down there you're in your coffin.'

'What's dangerous about it?' I asked, expecting him to mention sharks or the bends.

'You're down there by yourself.' He touched my arm. 'After two years I quit because I knew my luck was going to run out. Not much diving these days, anyway. It's all cultivated now.'

'What do you do now, then?'

'Break horses. What about you?'

'I'm just travelling around.' I told him about my trip and the Aboriginals I had met along the way. 'Most of them have been down and out,' I said.

'You probably spend too much time in pubs.'

Noticing a cross around his neck, I asked him if he was a Christian. 'I believe in a greater power,' he said. 'Some people call him Jesus. After my boxing career ended, I asked Jesus to give me another chance in life.' He saw I was sceptical. 'Put it this way, if God made our planet five miles closer to the sun, we wouldn't be here, or five miles further away and we'd be freezin'. See what I mean? You believe in him?'

'I'm not so sure.'

'He gave me a new life.' He stood close to me. His eyes were deep brown, and the whites were yellowed. He said emphatically, 'Don't ever be ashamed of yourself.'

'I try not to be.'

'Never!' he said.

166

lonely road home

In the afternoon I took a local bus to Cable Beach and walked along the widest beach I had been on in Australia, a stretch of unbroken whiteness whose popularity went a long way towards explaining Broome's tourist boom.

Back at the hostel, every nook and cranny was abuzz with young holiday-makers: girls in superfluous bikinis, stretching near the pool, or sitting on tall cane stools near the bar, smoking and laughing; self-conscious boys in florid board shorts and enormous runners and baseball caps. I resorted to my bunk. A couple of young men entered the dormitory shortly after, and, thinking I was asleep, shared a joint.

'I'm leaving,' said one. 'I've had absolutely no luck with the chicks here, man. So many gorgeous chicks.'

'What about Jody?'

'No, man. I don't know what it is with her.'

'You chase too hard, man. You've got to sit around, let 'em come to you.'

———

Port Hedland was six hundred kilometres down the coast with no town between it and Broome. There was a progression in the vegetation, from savannah to spinifex, a constant in the redness of the soil, whose only breach came a few hours out of Broome: a distant line of white dunes that reminded me we were still close to the sea. I saw no sign of life beyond a couple of roadhouses—no cattle, birds or kangaroos. Electricity pylons with drooping cables straddled the landscape. A railway track, the property of a mining company, gleamed in the afternoon sun. We passed a diesel engine pulling ninety-four empty ore carriages, returning to the Pilbara. Later in the day we reached some bare hills not much higher than the bus. And away to the right I saw dazzling white fields and white mounds that were part of a salt works in marshes near Port Hedland.

THE RED ISLAND

The contrast with Broome was extraordinary. Port Hedland was the antithesis of a tourist resort. The most obvious difference was the town's prevailing colour. It was a rusty pink, the result of years of shipping iron ore from its port. Everything was coated in an iron oxide dust—houses, shops, concrete footpaths, street signs, port facilities, even the clothes of its citizens. I tried to rub it off surfaces with my finger, succeeding with glass, but nothing else. The trees and grass were pink. The cheap hotel on the waterfront where I stayed was pink. So too, the slice of lemon that came with my fish and chips that evening, and not just its peel but its flesh, which I initially mistook for an over-ripe orange. The sea in the harbour channel had a red tinge, as if blood had been spilled. I climbed an observation tower behind the tourist office, and saw that all the roofs of shops and offices, all the buildings and cranes around the port, all the streets were pink, a grimy pink that transformed an industrial city into a parody. It could have been the set for a punk video clip. The tourists stayed away.

Perversely, I liked it, despite the sudden transformation of my clothes and skin. Port Hedland had a productive economic base: shipping iron to the world. I took a leisurely stroll around the filthy port and along the unremarkable foreshore, enjoying gusts of wind off the ocean, the first cool air I'd felt in two months. There was not a lot to do.

In the evening I went to a pub that was hosting a two-up tournament, the first I had seen. I talked to a ginger-bearded man, named Kirk, who worked in the kitchen at a local hospital. He explained the rules of play to me, and placed his bets with other spectators seated around a square formed from mooring rope. He shouted 'Head 'em up!' at the ringkeeper, and blinked nervously as the coins spun through the air. He had tremendous luck, but winning didn't seem to please him. He kept an eye on the crowd and surreptitiously pointed out a prostitute who had been in his room the night before.

lonely road home

I asked him about the pinkness of everything. 'If you wash your clothes in hot water,' he advised, looking at my jeans, 'you'll never get it out.' He told me most people prefer to live in South Hedland away from the grime of the port.

'Why would anyone live around here?' I asked. 'It doesn't seem to have a lot going for it.'

'Anyone who stays here has one thing in mind. Making money. You come up here for work. On the mines. In the port. Or in a job like mine. You don't come here for the comfortable lifestyle.' He chuckled at the thought. 'You put in a few hard years. Good wages, generally. You save your dough, and piss off. Back to Perth, Melbourne, Sydney, wherever you came from. And you've given yourself a bloody good start in life. Only most people get used to it up here, and never go back. The weather. The fishing. It may not be the prettiest of places, but the people here are good, hard-working bastards. They won't rip you off. They mind their own business. They'll help you out if you're in a spot of bother.'

———

I went to Cossack, a ghost town further down the coast at the mouth of the Harding River, built on bare iron-stone hills. Where the ground was flat, white grass flourished. The last few miles to the coast were along a causeway separating the river from a marshy flood plain.

Cossack had been the first port along this part of the coast, preceding Broome by twenty years. The first white settler, who arrived in 1863, named it Tien Tsin after the barque on which he ferried his stock, but later it was renamed to honour a governor who called at the port in *HMS Cossack*. Were it not for settlers noticing mother-of-pearl shell necklaces worn by local Aboriginals, the settlement might have remained an obscure outpost of the colony of Western Australia. A pearling industry burgeoned, and

THE RED ISLAND

the town was soon inhabited by Asian divers and merchants. It thrived for twenty years, until the pearlers shifted to Broome, after which it quickly returned to obscurity. But some of its stone buildings are still standing: the courthouse, the customs office, the post and telegraph building, the old police barracks and lock-up that is now a hostel.

I had a room with high ceilings and creaking floor boards to myself. I slept well and after breakfast I made a thorough inspection of the town. A museum, in the old courthouse, was full of fading photos of early landholders' families, and implements and devices that were testimony to the ingenuity of the isolated settlers. Opium pipes and revolvers revealed another side of Cossack life. I climbed Tien Tsin lookout for a wider view of the town. The buildings were a few hundred metres from the mouth of the Harding River, clustered around an intersection of gravel streets near the wharf. Behind Cossack the land was rough and undulating, covered in kapok grass. But across the wide river, mangroves extended over flat territory, land that had been worthless to the settlers.

There was something comforting about ghost towns, I mused. They were a reminder that things can change, that humans come and go, and that the world continues after they have gone. I walked out of Cossack along the road that led to Reader Head—a promontory protecting the mouth of the river—to the settlers' cemetery.

It told the usual stories of colonial life: high infant mortality rates, accidents and epidemics, the prevalence of cultural intolerance. I studied the Christian headstones then went further down the hill towards the estuary, to where the heathens were buried. And while I was studying the lovely vertical inscription on a slender Japanese tombstone, a distinctive bird song broke the silence. I traced it to a small pied bird perched in a scrawny bush nearby. It stopped singing as I approached, but it remained on its perch. I stared at it for

lonely road home

a while and it stared back, until I thought that one of us had to make a move before our encounter became uncanny. I walked away, up the hill. As I reached the road it began to sing again.

I kept following the road away from Cossack, towards the sea. The road rose and fell over small rocky hills. Low she-oaks and shards of iron-stone poked through kapok grass. At the end of the road, there was a lookout from which one could see a few small islands offshore, sand bars at the mouth of the river, stretches of white sand, and mangroves. As I climbed the final rise I heard a motor. On a distant decline a vintage black hearse was approaching. Dumbstruck, I watched, until it disappeared behind a hill. I waited for it to come over the next rise, thinking: *Jesus, it's coming for me!* I waited a good two minutes. Nothing showed. My relief was only restrained by my bewilderment. I sprinted to the lookout. The beach was a lovely white crescent with small breakers and blue water. Two figures on the sand were taking off their clothes. I looked behind the beach and saw a vehicle parked at the end of the road, a canary yellow van.

I returned to Cossack, hired a small motorboat from the man who ran the tea rooms, and sailed a little way offshore. I killed the motor, and for a while looked back at the land, thinking: *I'm so far from home, I'm starting to hallucinate.* The sea comforted me. I dropped my hand below its glimmering surface.

Late in the afternoon I left Cossack, hitching a ride to Wickham on the tray of an Aboriginal fisherman's ute, which I shared with his three young daughters. When I took my sun hat off to avoid losing it in the slipstream, they saw that I was bald, and a guessing game began.

'Thirty-one?'

'Older,' I confessed.

'He's four hundred.'

'No, he's not!'

THE RED ISLAND

'Fifty-six?'

'Younger.'

'Forty-six?'

'Forty-three,' I said.

'My dad's forty-five,' said one of them thoughtfully.

The three of them burst into song. 'Forever young! I want to be forever young!'

'You'll be as old as me before you know it,' I declared.

'Huh?' they chorused incomprehensibly. 'Forever young! Forever young!'

It was 4 a.m. when I arrived in Carnarvon, but representatives of the backpacker hostels were faithfully waiting to meet the bus. In the dark, they held up signs advertising friendliness and good times and freebies—free breakfast, free town shuttle service, free barbecues, free passes to the local disco—like the touts in Broome, Darwin, Alice Springs, Cairns, Hervey Bay, Byron Bay.

Carnarvon was a dreary town on a smelly sea inlet, a fishing port and rural service centre. Most of the hostel guests were seasonal workers or overnighters like myself. I went for a walk beside the inlet and along a sandy track through a stretch of mangroves to the open sea. Here I sat on a piece of driftwood and watched an assiduous eagle build a nest on top of a pilot stanchion. It was for such unexpected sights that I loved to travel.

I returned to town, but stayed outside on a park bench near the inlet and watched the sun descend behind a grey curtain of haze. And just as I was thinking it was time to eat, a flaccid man sat down beside me and, fidgeting with his plastic-rimmed sunglasses, gave me an uncertain smile. High blood pressure had caused his face to glow brighter than the tepid sunset. The skin was peeling off his nose, and his lips

lonely road home

had purple blisters. 'Can I sit here?' he asked apologetically.

He was dressed in a soiled ribbed body shirt and permanent press slacks that he had somehow managed to crease. He looked the diffident type, but for the next hour he talked to me—about how two nights earlier he had fled from a job at a roadhouse on the highway north of Carnarvon. He had been abused, accommodated in a sweatbox, and threatened with a knife. He had left his suitcase behind and hadn't collected his pay, walking along the fenceline parallel to the highway, until he collapsed in the heat and was found by a road worker. The police took him to hospital, where he spent a night under observation. In the morning the Salvation Army had supplied him with a ticket to Perth. And now he was scared to spend the night outdoors in Carnarvon, while waiting for the morning coach.

I suggested he stay at a hostel. He shrugged and fiddled with his glasses again. 'Don't have the money,' he confessed.

'Look, I'm going to eat,' I said. 'A hamburger. You're quite welcome to join me.'

'I bought some bananas with the last of my change.' He stood up and scratched his forehead, as if trying to remember something. 'I need to go to the toilet.'

It was quite dark now. The street lights had come on. And as he passed under the light near us, I noticed his fawn slacks ended above his ankles, leaving a fleshy gap between the cuffs and black socks. 'You know, at the roadhouse,' he said, 'they had a list on the wall in the office called *No-hopers Cup*. On it were the names of all the people who'd had my job, with comments next to them like, "couldn't handle a hard day's work," "likes little boys," "wouldn't know a petrol bowser from his prick." That sort of thing.' He sniggered or whimpered. 'My name'll be up there now, for sure.'

'There's a pub,' I said. 'It'll have a toilet.'

'It's a black pub,' he said, alarmed.

There were some Aboriginals going into the bar; others

THE RED ISLAND

hanging around outside. 'They won't stop you having a pee,' I said.

'Do you think it'll be safe at the bus stop tonight?'

'Jesus, it's just a small town,' I said, trying to reassure him. 'You could sleep in the middle of the street here and nothing would happen to you.'

I walked alone to the other end of the street and had a cheap and awful Chinese meal. As I headed back to the hostel I saw him at the bus stop. 'Did you find a toilet?'

'At a service station.'

'You going to be all right?'

He shivered. It was definitely getting cold. He put his hands in the pockets of his trousers. 'The bloke at the service station told me the only safe place to sit overnight was outside the cops.'

'Come back to the hostel,' I said, succumbing. 'I'll shout you a night.'

He followed me limply around the corner. To salvage a little of his pride, I handed him some money before we entered the office so it looked like he was paying his own way. I left him there and went to the living room to watch TV. Later he came over to give me my change. He had a bagful of freebies: plums from a tree in the yard and six eggs from the breakfast store that he had already boiled for the long trip to Perth. 'You want me to boil you some eggs?' he said.

By 7.15 a.m., I was on a mini bus for Monkey Mia. We travelled for an hour beneath a gossamer fog to the Peron Peninsula. I saw wild emus, stalking across red ground, taller than the scrub. The bus stopped in Denham, a coastal resort and Australia's most westerly town. So, I had been to the most easterly town, Byron Bay, and now to Denham on the other side of the continent. They couldn't have been less

lonely road home

alike. Denham was shabby and unpretentious, the air had a chill, the shoreline was unremarkable. On an island that I could see across the sound, Dirk Hartog had landed in 1616, the first officially recorded European on Australian soil.

We crossed the peninsula, an arid, rabbit-infested, desolate stretch of land, to Monkey Mia on Shark Bay, where the scene on the beach was remarkable, not least for the periodic visits of dolphins which swam into knee-deep water to interact with humans. There were caravans, chalets, tennis courts, as well as a restaurant and shops, right next to the sand. There was a jetty, from which large catamarans commenced tours of the bay to spot dugongs, and a boat ramp for anglers. There were yachts moored offshore. And along the beach, on the white sand, sat hundreds of patient tourists, awaiting a visitation.

The dolphins flouted regular hours. Some days they showed up at feeding time (although they didn't always eat); some days they wallowed in the shallows for hours; other days they didn't appear at all. But the tourists waited, as euphoric as cultists anticipating the second coming.

Their patience surprised me. When the dolphins arrived, the humans scrambled into the shallows to stare at them and touch them. And the curiosity was mutual, judging by the way these creatures tilted an eye above the surface to study the fence of legs at the edge of their world.

After two pleasant days at Monkey Mia, I caught a bus for Geraldton, crossing the definitive 26th parallel, then the Murchison River and undulating farmland—dried-out pastures, sheep, wheat crops, rows of trees planted as wind breaks, sturdy fences.

Geraldton was a port, reputedly the windiest town in Australia. It had towering silos by the sea, stone buildings

THE RED ISLAND

and Norfolk pines. I inspected its breakwaters and busy docks. I went to the maritime museum, which had items—cannons and navigational equipment—salvaged from the wreck of the *Batavia* that sank in 1629, eighty kilometres offshore.

Like most Australians I had heard the sinister tale of the *Batavia* that hit a reef in the northern Houtman-Abrolhos Islands. With little fresh water salvaged, and none on the barren island where the survivors had landed, the ship's commander had set out in a sloop to try to reach the wreck. In his absence a mutiny occurred, led by Jeronimus Cornelisz, a psychopath who ordered his followers to slaughter more than a hundred defenceless survivors. The mutiny was quashed when the commander returned, and all but two of the mutineers were brutally executed, losing their hands before they were hung. Two youngsters, Wouter Loos and Jan Pelgrom, were marooned on the mainland for their part in the slaughter, perhaps becoming Australia's first European immigrants. They disappeared without a trace.

Despite its familiarity, something about Geraldton seemed disjointed. There was a grandiose Catholic cathedral that seemed out of all proportion with the size of the town. And, in the main street, I was accosted by an evangelical window cleaner, who had found God when he twisted his ankle in a wheat field and cried out for help. As if to balance this abundance of piety, I saw neo-Nazi bikers in the street, and greaseballs whose cars bore stickers that flagged brazen messages: *A woman's place is on my face.*

Then, back at the hostel—a double-storey sandstone building, which used to be a hospital, and whose dormitories were old wards containing dozens of beds—half the guests seemed more like convalescents than backpackers. A group of intellectually disabled women were staying there with their carers. And an ancient man, so stooped that his nose dripped well in front of his feet, shuffled along the timber verandah and past my bunk with excruciating languor. The

lonely road home

women made cups of tea, watched television, or played cards in the living room, repeating routines they were used to, ignored by the backpackers around the pool table, who were mostly young blond surfers. When the old man managed to descend the stairs from his dormitory, he sat in an armchair with the others. Noticing he had taken a book by Dickens to read from the hostel's meagre library, I resolved to have a conversation with him.

I got my chance later in the afternoon. He was slumped on a cane seat outside his dormitory, playing a harmonica, his elbows perched on his hips to support the weight of the instrument, with only his lips and eyebrows moving. I stopped to listen to him, paid him a compliment when he finished, and asked him how many years he'd been playing. 'Only about seven,' he said in a wheezy voice, pleased when I expressed surprise.

'But you must be getting on,' I said. 'Late seventies?' I suggested, thinking he looked a hundred.

'I'm eighty-eight,' he said.

I asked if I could join him for a chat and pulled up a chair. 'Do you live here?'

'I'm a backpacker,' he said, and I almost burst into laughter. Then I was filled with admiration when I realised he was serious. It seemed incredible that someone so stooped and frail would call himself a backpacker, until an explanation for his stoop occurred to me: he had the posture of a retired coolie who had been carrying loads on his back, maybe a rucksack, all his life.

He was terribly thin. His body turned a right-angle below the chest, and another at the neck to keep his face vertical. His face was marked with sun spots, his eyes (one of them sightless) were sunken and moist, as if their sockets were the only parts of him that sweated. There were blue blisters on his lips and bruises on the backs of his sinewy hands. Yet, despite his decrepitude, his cardigan, trousers

THE RED ISLAND

and shoes were clean and neat, his face was shaved, his hair combed. His only oversight was to do without socks.

He told me his name was Charlie, and confirmed he was a compulsive traveller. Each year he left Sydney and travelled for four months, getting around on buses, staying in hostels. 'It's a bit harder these days. I can't walk too far. But all these backpacker places have their own mini buses, and they go around town each day.' On this year's trip he had been to Townsville, Charters Towers, Mount Isa, Katherine, Kununurra, Port Hedland, and now Geraldton, staying in each town for a week. To my amazement, he explained that he had some arrangement with his local Social Security office, which paid his accommodation bills. A bureaucracy that handled an old man's financial affairs while he travelled seemed too flexible, too compassionate, to actually exist. 'I used to work my way around,' he said. 'But not these days.'

'What sort of work?'

'Fencing, building dams, picking vegies, milking cows, wharfie, waiter, you name it,' he said. 'Last year I took a trip up to Cairns, then across to Croydon and Normanton. I was up that way, back in twenty-eight, twenty-nine, at the start of the depression. I once walked from Normanton down to Cloncurry. You been into the Gulf country?'

'I passed through Cloncurry,' I muttered in admiration.

'I used to jump trains in those days. On the susso we had ration cards, four pounds of meat, four pounds of bread, one pound of tea, that sort of thing, and you went to the police station to pick it up. But I used to register under different names all over the Gulf country, and then jump trains to get to each one.' His body shuddered with a silent chuckle. 'Got caught a couple of times. Spent twelve days in the lock-up at Croydon. Another twelve at Georgetown.'

'A hard life,' I said.

'I suppose so,' he answered. 'But it's what you're used to, isn't it? People say it's hard these days.'

178

lonely road home

He travelled alone. 'It's how you meet people. In Japan and later in Korea I got jobs teaching English by people tapping me on the shoulder.'

'You travelled in Japan and Korea?'

'A few years ago now.' He pursed his lips reflectively. 'And Thailand, Burma, India. I've been to Latin America.'

'Oh, where?'

'All over.' He had started at Rio, gone up the Amazon and into Bolivia, then on to Argentina and Chile. 'I picked peas outside Santiago.' Trips through Peru and Ecuador followed, then he went all the way to Mexico and into the USA.

'You must enjoy it.'

'Not always.'

'Why travel, then?'

'Staying in the one place,' he mused. 'That gets me down at times. When that happens I travel.'

In New Zealand he had worked on the wharves. 'And I used to edit a literary magazine there,' he said, wheezing. 'Called *Images*. Poetry mainly.'

Without prompting, he struggled to his feet and recited 'The Man from Snowy River' in a feeble drone, with his thumb tucked into the palm of one hand up near his chest, and his other hand pointing at the floor, a reciter's pose. Next came 'The Drover's Dream', which I had first heard performed to music by a piano-playing drunk at an aunt's soiree when I was a child. Finally, to prove his scope, he recited Rudyard Kipling's 'If'—only faltering once, from fatigue I assumed, in the final stanza.

'The funny thing was, while I was working on the wharves I met this Irishman, whose job was in the hold down near the ships' motors.' Apparently the engine noise allowed the Irishman to go into a trance, during which he could foresee the future. And he predicted that Charlie would be in a film about an incident that had happened two hundred years ago, dressed like a sailor. 'He also predicted

THE RED ISLAND

I'd never be rich. He was right on both accounts.' Charlie got a job on a yacht sailing to Tahiti. When he arrived, Hollywood was making *Mutiny on the Bounty* with Marlon Brando, Trevor Howard and Chips Rafferty. 'I got a job as a bit actor. I got to have a drink with Chips each evening. I wore a wig in the film. I was one of Fletcher Christian's men.' After Tahiti Charlie returned to Australia and went to work on the Ord River Scheme.

'I never had any luck with women, though,' he confided, telling me a long story about a girl he had met in New Zealand who broke his heart and prompted another man to suicide. 'Her name was Isa,' he said. 'The same as in Mount Isa in Queensland. Jeez, I remember that place when it was just a water tank, a few stone buildings, and a shaft in the ground. The tallest gum trees I've ever seen in Queensland used to grow round there. There's none left now.' He paused to think, his frail head nodding involuntarily. 'I never got married,' he whispered. 'Not after Isa.'

On the six-hour stretch to Perth, I sat next to a Greek who had immigrated to Australia thirty years ago. He said he loved the West for its climate and the fishing. 'It reminds me of where I come from,' he said. It was mid-October, but there was still some scrub in bloom. We travelled close to the coast, past wheat farms and sheep stations and through sturdy old townships built of sandstone.

In Perth I was met by two small septuagenarians. Uncle Rex was easily recognisable by his shining dome. His wife, Dorothy, had the same tight permed hair as his sister—my mother. I had met them only once before, when I was seven or eight, but we developed a rapport immediately. It occurred to me that I had reached the age that Rex had been at our first encounter.

lonely road home

In their back yard was a modern rotary clothes hoist, the sort that could be folded, uprooted and stored out of sight, a variation on the original that reflected a modern perception that the contraption was an eyesore. Inside their house were portraits of their family—children, grandchildren, a great grandchild—and two separate charts of photos, depicting family trees. I had seen most of Rex's photos before. My mother had them, and she'd had copies made for me. At the top was one of William Robinson whose grave I had visited in Rosedale on the second day of my trip. This chart explained why two old people in poor health would take a virtual stranger into their home, feed him, and behave like old companions.

In the next few days they showed me around Perth. We drove beside the Swan River, a lovely expanse of water that was as wide as a lake in places. We visited Kings Park above the city, and cruised the affluent suburbs overlooking the lofty north bank of the river, where the mansions looked like relics from the Roman Empire. The city centre, with its new office towers, sparkled in the distance. It had that squeaky clean look of Dallas, Texas, a dazzle that was sometimes blinding.

Later we had coffee in Fremantle, Perth's lovely historic port and Italian enclave, which the entrepreneur and yachtsman, Alan Bond, had spruced up for the defence of the America's Cup in 1987. Bond was awaiting trial on fraud and conspiracy charges, but Rex and Dorothy defended him ardently. 'Look at the good he's done for Perth,' Rex said. 'Bondy's not like some of them crooks, who only ever had their snouts in the trough for themselves.'

I liked Fremantle so much that, on a day when the public transport union was on strike, I walked ten kilometres from my uncle's place to the seaside suburb, mostly in a downpour that soaked me to the skin. I had a coffee in an Italian cafe, looking out at the wet old buildings across the street.

THE RED ISLAND

Eventually, the owner spoke to me, at first about the weather, then about herself. She had been in Australia since the fifties and loved Fremantle, its market and the sea, but she wanted her funeral to be in Napoli. I finished a second coffee. I couldn't stop shivering. 'You better go home. Dry off,' she advised. 'Or your funeral might be first.'

I was walking back in the rain when a car pulled up. 'Jump in boy,' shouted Rex, who had come looking for me. 'We thought you were lost.'

I shook the water off my useless poncho, and said, 'You're just in time to save my sense of humour.'

I was back to my winter clothes: beanie, t-shirt, shirt, windcheater, jacket, thick socks, boots. I had been travelling for more than three months, mostly in the tropics. Now I was experiencing weather that made me feel at home. I headed south as far as Albany, where hills ranged into the sea, forming islands across King George Sound. The town had been a whaling port until treaties put an end to the international trade in blubber. The whaling station at Cheynes Beach ceased operating in 1978. And the port these days depended entirely on the export of farming produce. An arm of land curled around to protect the town from the worst of the weather, but the sea was still choppy and grey.

I travelled the rest of the day to Esperance, through flowering scrubland with mountains to the north, then fields of wheat and canola, and pastures where sheep grazed. High clouds, the colour of ice, arched across the sky. The bus was half empty. This corner of Australia seemed almost as remote as the north. As we approached the Fitzgerald River National Park—a wide depression in the landscape—a woman sitting in front of me spoke to her neighbour: 'It's

lonely road home

very Australian, isn't it?' I wondered what she was expecting.

I stayed a night in Esperance, a grain port on another wild stretch of coast. Then I headed inland to Kalgoorlie.

———

The Eastern Goldfields had a fabulous history: I had heard stories of miners bathing in champagne because it was cheaper than water, and how the town of Norseman was named after a horse which kicked over a nugget of gold. 'It's still a one-horse town,' quipped Meredith, a journalist I met in Kalgoorlie. She sauntered into the bar from another section of the pub where she had been drinking with members of the Gold Stealing Squad, a branch of the Kalgoorlie police whose purpose was to ensure that every ounce of gold extracted from the earth was accounted for.

'That's an ambiguous title,' I said.

She scratched her wispy hair and gave the faintest of smiles. 'There's nothing ambiguous about those guys.' While waiting for an alcoholic soda, she invited me to join her at a table with some friends. 'Friends as distinct from associates,' she said. 'In a town like this, you quickly learn the importance of drinking with both.'

Two of her friends, Jane and Sally, were lawyers. Carl was a geologist. Sally asked me what I thought of Kalgoorlie, and when I told her I was impressed, she said, 'Have you seen the skimpies yet?'

The skimpies turned out to be scantily dressed barmaids who for a tip would expose their tits. 'It's one of the cultural events of Kalgoorlie,' Carl explained. 'They're at the Exchange at certain hours or at the pub up the top end. Essential sight-seeing.' It seemed rather tame entertainment in Australia's most notoriously licentious city, famous for its gaudy brothels.

'My boyfriend always drinks at a skimpy bar,' said Sally,

183

THE RED ISLAND

sounding like she was admitting to personal failure. 'So I meet him there sometimes. Personally, I wouldn't do that sort of work.' Talk of her boyfriend had her emptying her glass. 'I've got to go. He gets jealous if I turn up late.'

'Kalgoorlie's changed a lot,' Carl said, 'but it hasn't entirely shaken off its ribald past. The brothels are still here, doing a healthy trade in Hay Street. Where you've got mines, you've got brothels.'

'I dunno about a healthy trade,' said Meredith.

Carl had expressive eyebrows and a tiny beard on his bottom lip. He had been born in Germany and, although he had lived in Australia most of his life, he hadn't lost his accent entirely. 'We should show you around,' he suggested.

We walked along Hannan Street to the York Hotel, which had a lofty pressed-metal roof and an exquisite interior staircase and decor. Despite its reputation, Kalgoorlie was an elegant city. I had already wandered many of its streets, admiring the buildings, an inordinate number of which were hotels. 'Mining's a thirsty business, too,' said Carl, 'especially in this sort of country. Tomorrow you can see what it's like. If you want, I'll take you out of town.'

The next afternoon, Carl and Meredith drove me to the Golden Mile, once a tract of mine headframes and winches and corrugated-iron miner's huts, now a vast cavity surrounded by stark pyramids of tailings. There were seams and holes in the earth wall where cross-cuts and old shafts had been exposed. 'The underground mines were going broke,' Carl said. 'Kalgoorlie was facing ruin. The last big commercial operation was literally within hours of closing when a new technique for extracting gold was announced. It saved everyone's bacon. That and the price of gold going up.'

The result was an open-cut mine of such massive proportions that the earthmoving vehicles creeping up a zigzag road on the far wall below looked the size of toys.

lonely road home

We drove through Boulder, Kalgoorlie's poor relation, then out into the country. The land around Kalgoorlie was lusher than I expected. We headed west to Coolgardie, a boom town less fortunate than Kalgoorlie, whose grand old buildings seemed sadly out of place. North of Coolgardie the scenery delighted me: slender green-trunked eucalypts, meadows of purple then yellow, flocks of insouciant emus and, in the cloudless sky, patiently circling eagles. 'You're seeing it at its best,' Carl declared. Plentiful rain could give arid regions a brief period of brilliance. And in the midst of this loveliness were ruins, the walls and chimney of an old stone building, more than likely a hotel. Outside some joker had erected a sign: *Skimpy tonite "Mm Mm" Meridick*.

'So this is where you moonlight it,' I said to Meredith.

'My objection to skimpies,' she said, 'is that there are no male ones.'

An hour or so later we arrived at a slightly more substantial community called Ora Banda whose pub at least had a roof on it. In fact it had a barmaid, several customers and a few sleeping dogs. Ora Banda had once been a town of 2000 or more; now fewer than fifty people still lived there. Some of the drinkers looked like they had been residents since its heyday, but I fell into a conversation with a more recent arrival, a chubby miner with a missing canine tooth.

'I'm like Bondy. A bankrupt,' he said, answering my question about what had brought him here. 'I used to run a trucking business over in Sydney. Had to leave there quick, mate. A lot of angry employees wanted my blood.' For eighteen months he had been working underground in Ora Banda, earning $90,000 a year. The barmaid came over. 'Hey Sue, why aren't there any skimpies working here?' he lamented.

'There's plenty of flesh shown around here as it is.' She turned to me, the stranger, to explain. 'You often see naked men in this pub.'

THE RED ISLAND

'There you go, Meredith,' I said. 'They have male skimpies here.'

Sue gave me a wink, and called to a bearded old-timer in a felt hat who was hunched on a stool at the far end of the bar. 'Hey, Ted, naked men slide around on the floor here all the time, don't they?'

'Why ask me?' he answered gruffly.

'Are you one of them?' I called.

'Shit no.'

'If it's your birthday,' Sue said, 'you're allowed to slide around in your birthday suit.'

It was late in the afternoon. Carl drove his Land Rover along a narrow dirt road to Broad Arrow, whose only remaining permanent structure was a corrugated iron shed: the hotel. My guide book said, 'Broad Arrow now has a population of 20, compared with 2400 at the turn of the century, but one of the town's original hotels operates in a virtually unchanged condition.'

A couple of young miners, in flannel shirts and filthy jeans, were drinking in the bar, chatting to a thin sullen barmaid. There was graffiti on the grimy walls and ceiling. We went into a back room, which had a small pool table and a couple of old framed photos on a wall. I headed into the adjoining urinal. *Why look up here,* said a sign near the ceiling, *when the joke is in your hand.*

When we stepped outside, the light was diminishing. Parked near the Land Rover was a ute without a windscreen. 'Once, outside this pub,' said Meredith, 'I saw a guy pissing on the engine of someone's car. He got into a fight with his dick hanging out.'

On the way back into town, we detoured onto a maze of dirt tracks through scrub, until we reached a battered corrugated-iron circular compound where a two-up school was held. It had a grim atmosphere. Thirty or forty people were betting, as much as a hundred dollars a throw, and

lonely road home

muttering, 'Head 'em up!' or 'Tail 'em up!' This school was famous throughout Australia. 'The governor was on his way here once when it was still illegal,' Meredith said. 'The cops were planning a raid on the same night. Apparently the governor was just warned in time.'

They forgot to show me Kalgoorlie's famous brothels. With a few idle hours the next morning, I strolled down to Hay Street. The brothels were closed at that hour, a long row of sheds with pink cement-sheet facades, each decorated with dainty hearts, pictures of naked girls, erotic messages. A woman stepped out of a taxi and ducked into one of the sheds without taking much notice of me. But the writing on a board outside her room was different: *Most know how to be silent. Few know when.*

———

Until a few decades ago the trip across the Nullarbor Plain was one of the world's great automotive adventures: a thousand miles of sandy track with only a few roadhouses along the way. Work to seal the road was completed in 1976, but the crossing could still be risky. Recently, floods had cut the highway leaving cars and road transports stranded for a week.

I had wanted to see the Nullarbor Plain even if it was from the highway which skirted its southern edge. The best way to cross it was by train, but I planned to make one more major detour before I went home—to Coober Pedy in South Australia—and that would drain the last of my funds. The train was out, and the coach only travelled at night. I would leave Kalgoorlie in the afternoon and wake up the next day 1200 kilometres away at the eastern edge of the plain.

Despite my disappointment, I was glad to be heading east, heading towards home. My coccyx ached. I missed Tania. And I was beginning to miss Melbourne.

THE RED ISLAND

The coach left Kalgoorlie at 3.30 p.m. At sunset we were passing the pink shores of small salt lakes near Norseman. We had a meal break at a roadhouse, my final stop in Western Australia. In the early hours of the next day we crossed the border into South Australia, near the lonely community of Eucla. By dawn we were travelling through empty grasslands, sheep country without a sheep in sight.

I broke my journey in Ceduna and spent the day walking around the shore. I rang Tania to tell her I would be home in a week, then sat in a motel bed and watched TV late into the night. The coach I caught the next morning was the worst I had travelled on in Australia. My seat stank of stale urine. The arm rests and interior coverings were worn through to the metal. The bus's gearbox whined and whistled. 'The one blessing,' I wrote in my notebook, 'is that the video is broken too.' All day we travelled through sunny wheat fields, with patches of scrub occasionally breaking the monotony. At Kimba, an ugly little town ('halfway across Australia', if you could believe the signs), a giant statue of the enemy of all wheat farmers, the galah, had been erected in accordance with the philosophy that it is better to be remembered for something hideous than nothing at all.

Around Kimba the wheat still had a green tinge. The fields were as uniform as the sea, with every little hill a scrubby island. Harmless high clouds stretched across the sky, towards a distant blue range.

As we approached the range, the colour fragmented into greens and reds. What looked like lofty mountains became a ridge of hills whose height was exaggerated by the flatness of the fields. The green, too, was deceptive. I mistook it for pasture. But it was scrub, gleaming in the afternoon light. The red was bare rock, an open-cut mine that was reducing the range to the level of the plain. This was Iron Knob, Australia's oldest iron-ore mine, a gaping legacy of our economic fortunes. Whyalla was near here, a port and a steel-

lonely road home

producing town. It was South Australia's second largest city but, with a population under 30,000, the coach by-passed it.

After Iron Knob we descended into a shallow valley, the extension of Spencer Gulf, to Port Augusta, where I left the bus at a roadhouse to await another heading north. With six hours to kill, I walked several kilometres into the centre of the town, across a causeway where the concentration of salt in the shallow sea had turned the water pink. Away to the east were the lovely Flinders Ranges, but on the causeway the skyline was dominated by a power station belching gases over the gulf. Port Augusta surprised me. It had a small central park that reminded me of towns in Latin America. And the resemblance didn't stop there: besides its name having a Hispanic resonance, the buildings ended abruptly two blocks from the centre, where Spencer Gulf was no more than an unremarkable inlet, and on the badlands between the town and the stinking water was a railhead with a few abandoned carriages and boxcars. It was like a scene from Patagonia, with all its hopelessness, thwarted ambition, ineptitude.

I was asleep within minutes of leaving Port Augusta and woke at five the next morning, six hundred kilometres away in Coober Pedy. I wanted to see the part of Australia that had been viewed by more people around the world than any other (Uluru, Sydney Harbour Bridge and the Opera House included), thanks to the Mad Max movies.

A mini bus arrived at the terminal and took me back to a hostel where I was led downstairs to a dormitory, one of a series of roughly hewn caverns underground. I slept for two hours, then climbed out of the clammy hole to stretch my legs on the surface.

Coober Pedy was like no other town on earth. The place had no vegetation to speak of, and the white ground—grit

THE RED ISLAND

rather than soil—glared even in the feeble light of dawn. It hurt my eyes and had me reaching for my sunglasses. The grit was everywhere. It threatened to bury the town's few bitumen roads. It formed large mounds on vacant land. Those buildings not carved into the low hills seemed plastered with it. And soon it was in my shoes, the pockets of my jeans, my underwear, beneath my collar, sticking to my skin as if I had been wallowing in it. The mounds on vacant land were mullock heaps, the tailings of opal mines—the original diggings—around which the town had burgeoned. Most of Coober Pedy was underground, and what wasn't looked as though it ought to have been. I climbed the hill behind the hostel, which gave me a view in all directions, from where the scattered buildings, many surrounded by piles of rusting junk, looked makeshift and derelict.

It was a different story underground. Despite their shabby exteriors, many of the shops, restaurants, hotels, and even churches carved into the earth were stylish and comfortable once you had passed through their doors and along their entrance shafts. It was as though the principles of architecture had been subverted by local Dadaists who insisted that functional space in the Antipodes be located in excavations, and foundations pushed into the air.

The reason for building underground, however, was somewhat more prosaic. This region had one of the most inhospitable climates in Australia, with temperatures in summer never dropping below 46°C. In late October, while I was there, the daytime temperature rose each day to the high thirties. In the epoch before air-conditioning it seemed infinitely more sensible to live underground where the temperature remained a constant 23°C. Obsolete mines were modified and transformed into residences, which the locals called 'dugouts'. Some were as big as forty squares, with indoor pools, spas and gyms. Extensions were simply a matter of bringing the drilling rig home from work.

lonely road home

Although air-conditioned houses had been built on the surface, the most prized real estate in town was still found underground.

In the afternoon, while I was having a beer at the Italo-Australia Club on the hill in the middle of town, I met a retired miner whose name was Jack, a silver-headed Australian (there was not an Italian in sight) with enormous hands and a generous girth. 'I was a miner for twenty-six years,' he said. 'But now I've told me boys I'm taking it easy.' He told me he was originally from Port Pirie, on Spencer Gulf, where he had owned a newsagency. 'I come up here for a holiday with a mate. It took us four days to get here. The road was almost non-existent. We were only intending to stay a week,' he chuckled. 'A new field was just starting up. We bought a hundred and fifty sticks of gelignite. We were terrified. We didn't realise you had to go down twenty metres. Fourteen days later, much to the disgust of the wife, we found twenty thousand dollars worth of opal, which was a lot of money in those days. Needless to say, we got the opal fever. The wife said, "If you build a dugout I'll stay a year." As you can see, I'm still here. And so's the wife. Must have something to do with how I've kept me good looks.'

'Nothing to do with the fortune you've made?' I guessed.

'Shit no!'

When he stopped laughing, I asked him what Coober Pedy was like when he first arrived.

'At that particular time there was no police, no TV, no radio. It was a pretty wild place. Brawls and gunfights. Jeez, it was fun though, and the police came and spoiled everything. No, not really. They had to come. There were no services here like there are today. And they used to have to truck in water. There were 600 men in Coober Pedy, forty Australians, the rest ethnics. If you heard English you whipped around and thought, "Jesus, who said that?" Later

THE RED ISLAND

on, after a big opal strike, three thousand men from the Andamooka fields came here in a month.'

'They don't still truck the water in, surely?'

'The government stepped in, put a bore down, and built a big filtration plant to get rid of the salt. Listen, how would you like to have a look around?'

He took me to one of the opal fields a few kilometres out of town. On the way we passed a football ground whose grassless surface was rocky and hard. 'We bring 'em up tough here,' he said. The golf course was even more barren: dusty ill-defined fairways and, instead of greens, 'scrapes', which I had also seen in the Northern Territory and Western Australia, oil-soaked patches of smooth earth. Jack had a respectable handicap. He mentioned that the town had a racetrack too.

'Turf?' I asked.

'As much as you see here on the golf course,' he replied. 'There's one meeting a year, a big three-day piss up.'

In half a day I had become rather blase about the barren landscape of Coober Pedy, but that changed the moment we reached the Olympic opal field. 'Named by the Greeks who put down the first claim here,' Jack said. 'A mate of mine sunk a shaft one day and overnight the Greeks claimed it. They struck one of the richest seams ever found.' One of fifty fields, Olympic was two kilometres wide and twelve kilometres long, containing half a million shafts, each with its white mullock heap like a giant gopher mound and not a blade of vegetation in sight.

As Jack drove between them, away from the road, not following any track that I could discern, I experienced sensory deprivation of a sort. All I could see were holes less than a metre in diameter, occasional caravans and crane-like machinery, and intimidating mounds of disgorged earth. 'Some blokes stay near their mines all the time to stop thieves coming in overnight,' he said. 'When you see a

192

lonely road home

caravan near a shaft, you know the bugger down below's on a good strike.'

Jack arrived at his latest shaft like an ant guided by instinct to its nest. 'I only go down occasionally now,' he said. 'It's the boys' turn to make a bit.'

'Do women mine?'

'Women have claims. But that's because you're only allowed one claim at a time. If the wife has a claim, I can work two, right? Mine and hers. I don't know of any women who go underground. It's bloke's work.'

Partnerships were as sophisticated as business arrangements got in Coober Pedy. There were no operational mining companies to speak of. Surprisingly, the South Australian government proscribed them, allowing only individuals who could afford a small licence fee and the initial capital outlay for equipment, perhaps $40,000, to take their chances. It was risky, but there was nothing Australians liked more than a gamble. 'Ninety-nine out of a hundred holes don't contain opals,' Jack said. 'And it's dangerous, particularly if you've got the fever. Once it nearly cost me my life while I was working a nice green and orange band. The ground talks to you. It groans like an old ship. It warns you. But I couldn't give up this band. I had the opal fever. The greed gets you, you see, makes you think all strange, makes your eyes roll around. It's a madness. My partner came and warned me. But I just kept working. And the ground was groaning. Twenty minutes later I was buried. I'm one of the few to survive a cave-in. A lot of blokes have lost their lives here.'

'How do you know where to sink a shaft?' I asked.

'Throw your hat into the air. Where it lands, start digging.'

Later in the afternoon I learnt that the contractor who did the mail run from Coober Pedy to Oodnadatta and William Creek took a few tourists with him twice a week in a ten-seat air-conditioned Land Cruiser to supplement his

THE RED ISLAND

income, a twelve-hour trip that covered six hundred kilometres. Thinking it was my only chance to visit Oodnadatta, a town whose name had intrigued me since childhood, I joined the run the following morning with three retired Sydneysiders, Mavis, Lorna and Reg. The mailman was John, a robust man with neat hair and a steely handshake, who had lived in Coober Pedy for twelve years. The mail run was an expansion of his business interests and a diversion from the mining. 'We're a strange breed of people, us miners,' he said. 'Every bugger for himself. But if the community needs something we all pull together. We raised enough for a fire engine in a night of two-up.'

'Who buys the opals?' Mavis asked, as we headed out of town.

'Chinese opal dealers,' he said. 'They live in hotels in Coober Pedy, then spend a few months selling in Hong Kong. They drive a hard bargain, too. And if you get the price you want, they whisper, "Don't tell anyone I gave you that price." You might want three hundred dollars and they say two forty-five. They won't move. So you say two fifty plus a carton of beer, and they're off to the bottle shop in a flash.'

'Saving face is important to them,' said Mavis, who had spent a king's ransom saving hers.

We were out of Coober Pedy and on a smooth gravel track beyond the clutter and the mullock heaps. 'I don't suppose any of yers pay taxes,' said Reg, sniggering. 'I mean, how would the tax man keep a trace of what you're digging up and selling?'

'If you don't pay taxes, and you're not on the dole, they wonder where you get your money from.'

'Still you wouldn't have to declare everything, would yers?' insisted Reg, whose lower eyelids drooped as loose and raw as a bloodhound's. 'I mean, if you had any brains, you wouldn't.'

We passed through the Dog Fence which crossed

lonely road home

Australia diagonally from near Surfers Paradise in Queensland to somewhere on the coast near Ceduna. 'It's almost six thousand kilometres long,' John said. 'The longest artificial barrier in the world, and probably the most pointless.' Its purpose was to contain dingoes to the north-west of the continent away from sheep country. But there were dingoes on both sides; I had seen plenty of them, myself, in Victoria.

John stopped long enough for us to take photos of the wire-netting barrier, which snaked along a low orange ridge towards the horizon in both directions. The sky was hazy. The morning air was warm and pleasant. The ground was absolutely bare.

Except for sand dunes along the coastline, I had never seen land without some vegetation, at least some withered spinifex or saltbush. Here nothing grew. Just after the Dog Fence we crossed Moon Plain. Its sharp rocky surface, for as far as I could see, glimmered in the sun as if scattered with sequins.

I stared engrossed in the desolate scenery, and spotted an anomaly two hundred metres from the track, a forty-four gallon drum standing alone, the same colour as the earth.

For the next hour we crossed Moon Plain until we reached a dry creek bed, Giddi Giddina, which coursed to parched Lake Cadibarrawirracanna. The landscape changed a little, with scrawny bushes defining its banks, and then another plain with enough soil to hold down clumps of withered grass. A low range in the distance dispelled the sensation that the earth was flat. There were two more creeks, Algebullcullia and Lora, which were distant tributaries of the great salt expanse of Lake Eyre. We crossed both before we reached the range. It was difficult to imagine water sluicing these crude channels, but periodic violent storms transformed them into dangerous torrents. The land endured extremes, as if no other possibility existed.

THE RED ISLAND

People lived out here. Aboriginals had hunted for millennia around these creeks. And over near the hills was Mount Barry cattle station, the mailman's first stop. 'This one's owned by the Williams family,' John said. The land around had only marginally more vegetation than Moon Plain, but enough apparently to keep cattle alive. 'They supply most of the beef to the Woolworths chain. They freight their cattle down to a property near Port Augusta to fatten them up before they're slaughtered. Woolworths are pretty fussy.'

I was amazed at how ordinary the Mount Barry homestead seemed: a solid house with a neat garden, sheds, outhouses and water tanks. An urbane young woman came out to greet John, and a farm hand came over from one of the sheds to help unload some boxes from the trailer. The young woman answered our questions: Yes, it was isolated, but she liked it like that. No, she didn't get lonely. Yes, she sometimes worried about how the isolation affected her children, but they had a chance each year to spend time with other children they knew in Port Augusta. Yes, she went to the city now and then. No, she wouldn't want to live there. She loved station life.

Her children had a classroom in one of the farm buildings. But their teacher was 600 kilometres away in Port Augusta, at the school of the air, which transmitted lessons to outback children by two-way radio. In Mount Isa I had visited a similar school and sat in on a lesson in a studio. Squeaky voices had filled my earphones as grade-one students responded dutifully to their teacher's questions. Students in the same class could be 1000 kilometres or more apart. On many remote properties mothers supervised their children's schoolwork, but the students at Mount Barry Station had an assistant.

She showed me the students' workbooks and explained the day's lesson. One of the students, a friendly child who told me her name was Elizabeth, showed me her latest

lonely road home

paintings and a prized possession, a photograph of herself with Sam Neill and William Hurt, who had visited her one day on a break from filming *Until the End of the World* near Coober Pedy.

After Mount Barry, Reg asked how one station knew its cattle from the rest.

'They brand them,' John said. 'But there's an old saying around here: if you want a feed of your own beef, you go to your neighbour's for tea.'

He asked if any of us had been to Oodnadatta.

'I have,' said Reg. 'Back in 1943.'

John looked at him through the rearview mirror. 'It won't have changed much,' he said.

'Come up on the Ghan during the war,' Reg added, mentioning the Adelaide to Alice Springs train that used to run through Oodnadatta. 'A big Abo with a wad of chewing gum behind his ear, that's what I remember of the place.'

'It's mainly an Aboriginal community now. After the old Ghan line closed, the whites left. It's not too badly run, though.'

It took another hour and a half through the meagre scrub to get there. As we crossed Neales Creek on the edge of town, John pointed to a soak where a Chinese market garden had grown at the turn of the century. 'There was gold out this way, so the Chinese were here,' John said. 'So were the Afghans.' Before the railway was extended north, Oodnadatta had been an important railhead. The Afghans drove camels to Alice Springs before the train that assumed their name supplanted them.

The rail, like the Great Overland Telegraph Line, had followed an ancient Aboriginal trade route along a series of permanent springs. The problem for the railway (and the reason it had been relocated further west by 1980) was that it traversed a flood plain. Those violent storms could turn the region into an inland sea in a matter of hours, often

THE RED ISLAND

washing away the track and stranding passengers for weeks at a time.

'Have you heard the one about the pregnant woman on the Ghan?' said John, assuming the earnest tone of a joker. 'She starts to have contractions and asks the conductor how long to Alice Springs. He says, "Pregnant women shouldn't travel on the Ghan." To which she replies, "I wasn't pregnant when I boarded."'

'This is a very emotional moment for me,' said Reg softly, seriously scanning the view for the first time.

'There's not much left of the old railway,' said John. 'They've ripped most of it up now. The station's still there. They turned it into a museum.'

John drove around the town, past a roadhouse painted pink, an Aboriginal community centre in a corrugated-iron building, decorated with a modern mural, the Railway Museum, the pub. 'Old bloke once brought some cattle into Oodnadatta,' he said. 'After he sold them, he decided to have a beer. He propped on a stool in the pub for four days. Then the cop came along and said, "You've had enough, I'll drive you home." Home was four hours away. And when the cop got back to Oodnadatta he needed a beer himself. He went into the pub, and there was the old bloke propped on the same stool. As soon as the cop had dropped him off at home, the old bugger got straight in his plane and flew back.'

As he returned to the roadhouse, I saw a yard piled high with the wrecks of motor vehicles. 'The Oodnadatta School of Driving,' John muttered.

Everything about the roadhouse was pink—its exterior and interior, its workshop, the jeep, the tractor and canoes. Canoes? The ground was bare and orange, and the light was brutal to any unshaded eyes. John tried to explain the road-house's colour scheme. The owners had reached Oodnadatta on a camel safari twenty years earlier. 'The last of the sixties hippies,' he said.

lonely road home

Lorna had a more practical theory. 'Pink paint was going cheap.'

We ate inside, served by a young Irish woman, who told me she had been in Oodnadatta for five years. I wondered what possessed a native of the greenest land on earth to stay in a place where grass never grew. She had just been passing through and fell in love with it. 'It was like I had found my real home.'

After a hamburger I walked around in the heat. I was pleased with myself. I had reached Oodnadatta, accomplishing a lifetime ambition. It was not the prettiest place on earth, but travel is best when it's the pursuit of what kindles your imagination. A name, a photo, a tale. I went as far as the railway station, where a couple of Aboriginal youths were ambitiously landscaping the ground near tracks that were disappearing beneath the shifting Oodnadatta soil. Reg came along, assisted by Lorna, and stood staring at the sandstone station building. 'Jesus Christ,' he muttered. 'It seems like only yesterday.'

As his bloodhound eyes began to moisten, Lorna comforted him. 'There, there,' she said, patting his back.

Once John had finished his mail duties at the roadhouse, we headed south towards William Creek, following the Oodnadatta track or the 'string of springs', and the old Ghan line. 'If the old tracks could talk!' John shouted above the noise of the tyres on the dirt road.

'During the war,' Reg said, 'I was posted to an isolated spot up near Darwin. Came up to the Alice by train. Then we were all put on bloody old trucks. You can't imagine the dust. And red! Jesus, it stuck to yer clothes, yer skin, yer hair, everthin'. We looked like bloody Abos by the time we got there. I was there till the war ended. Radio operator, I was. Lost me hearing listening to static in the earphones.'

'Haven't things changed since the war,' Mavis declared. 'When you think of the number of babies that used to die!'

199

THE RED ISLAND

'Children used to die of all sort of things you don't even hear of now,' Lorna added. 'Polio. Whooping cough.'

'Big changes,' said Reg. 'They don't use morse code any longer.'

'You remember them old bath heaters,' said Lorna.

'The old coppers?' shouted John. 'We still had one of those when I was a kid.'

'I can still remember the first washing machine I ever used,' said Lorna.

'Remember the kerosene fridges?' said John.

'Look there's the railway again,' called Reg. 'I guess I've been along here before.'

'If you travelled on the Ghan,' said John without bothering to complete the sentence.

We stopped to look at an old rusting pump house and water tower, standing starkly on a desert plain amongst fallen timber beams, and sheets of corrugated-iron roofing scattered by the wind. The rails and the sleepers were gone, but the ground where the track had been laid was raised enough for me to trace its path towards the Algebuckina Bridge, a five-hundred metre steel span across a wide soggy creek bed. Reg went to the start of it, took a few hesitant steps, then retreated.

I saw some wild goats in the scrub on the other side of the creek and pointed them out to John. 'In the days when the Ghan got stranded for a week or more at a time, the train driver used to shoot the goats to feed his passengers,' he said. 'There's camels here as well, and you might see a dingo or two.'

I did see two dingoes, but that was when we were almost to William Creek just before sunset, after stopping at two more stations along the way, meeting the women at the homesteads and the children in their private classrooms. I spotted the dingoes in the distance, so white I thought they were sheep. When they moved I knew what they were. They

lonely road home

padded insouciantly across an open expanse that was turning red with the sun's descent, confident, handsome canines, undaunted by our presence.

We stopped for a snack in the pub at William Creek while John delivered mail to its seven or so inhabitants. Outside was the owner's small aeroplane, not far from a parking meter and a huge cylindrical piece of space junk that had apparently been launched in the sixties from Woomera, 400 hundred kilometres away to the south. The pub was built of cement sheet and corrugated iron, with a sign declaring it was the gateway to the Simpson Desert and Lake Eyre.

'Did my harmonica come?' called the owner's young son when he saw John. He sorted through a pile of letters and parcels. The owner's aviation magazines were there and so was some junk mail for the English barmaid.

'How did they get my name?' she complained.

The owner's wife was pregnant, and her father, a beet-root-faced portly man, was helping out with the chores. He had just managed to blackout the electricity supply to the caravan park behind the hotel with an electrical appliance he was supposed to have repaired. He went to serve Mavis who wanted a gin and tonic. 'Oh, you're back,' he said, in an oblique slur on tourists. 'Only you've changed yer dress.'

Mavis frowned. 'I've never been here before,' she declared. 'But my nephew has. He told me he'd pinned his licence to your ceiling. He wanted me to see if it was still up there.'

'You're welcome to look for it,' he grinned.

There must have been several hundred licences or ID cards stuck to the ceiling above us. 'Where to start?' she mused.

There were a few other customers in the bar. I tried to interest a chubby worker in conversation. He was wearing a navy singlet and dirty khaki shorts. He told me he was based in Marree, and had been grading the Oodnadatta and

THE RED ISLAND

Birdsville Tracks for seventeen years. It had obviously affected his capacity for small talk. Noticing his pained expression,
I desisted.

It was dark by the time we left. John had one more call to
make, Anna Creek station. Covering more than 30,000
square kilometres, it was largest cattle station in the world,
owned by the Kidmans, Australia's most famous cattle
family. 'It has eighteen thousand head of cattle,' said John.
'When I told that to an upper-class Pommie one trip, she
said, "Oh, good heavens, do they count them every morning?" That was one or two cattle per square mile. John
chuckled. 'You've got to laugh at the Poms. Don't get me
wrong, I like them. One day, come five o'clock, I stopped the
bus and said, "That's it. I don't work after five. The union
says, no work." "What happens to us?" they said. You
should've seen their poor bloody faces. I said, "Not my problem, mate."'

Anna Creek station homestead was poorly lit when we
arrived. We stayed in the vehicle while John delivered the
last of his mail. All of us were feeling weary. We had been
travelling for nine hours, and still had 200 kilometres to go.

'You wouldn't spot an Abo on the road, now,' said Reg,
peering into the darkness when we returned to the track.

'Only his eyes as the bull bar hit him,' sniggered Lorna.

'Do the Abos cause much trouble in town?' asked Reg.

'Coober Pedy's too tough,' predicted Mavis. 'They'd get
a hiding.'

'You give 'em all this land,' said Reg. 'And what do they
do? Drift into the towns and make a nuisance of themselves.'

'What gets me,' interjected Mavis, 'is how there's signs up
saying Aboriginal Land, and they won't let you in unless
you've got a permit.'

'Where do you live?' I asked.

'North Ryde,' she said. A cosy Sydney suburb.

'Do they need permission to get into your home?'

lonely road home

'Don't be ridiculous,' she tutted. 'It's not the same thing, is it?'

———

The next day I skulked around Coober Pedy, wanting to leave. But the bus to Adelaide wasn't due until midnight. I sat in a cafe and drank coffee. In the afternoon, I took a short tour around the town, which included a visit to the Big Winch tourist lookout, an underground church, the Jupiter Opal Field, a 'noodling' area where tourists scoured abandoned mullock heaps for opals, and Crocodile Harry's dugout.

Crocodile Harry was one of the region's most famous tourist attractions. 'He's partial to young women,' our guide said. 'Also, he might be pissed when we get there. We'll still be able to have a good look around though.'

Crocodile Harry's dugout was like a series of caves. It had been his mining site, which had reputedly yielded a fortune in opals. It was dug into the side of a hill rather than sunk vertically into the ground. Outside in a tiny quarry were the wrecks of three car bodies, which had been converted into garden beds where weeds, creepers, and mature cacti grew. Marcel Duchamp would have felt at home here amongst the collection of readymades that decorated the quarry wall: a misplaced bicycle wheel, an aeroplane propeller, a seat suspended in the air. Behind a container wall there was a pile of beer bottles as tall as a mullock heap. But it wasn't until I had followed the other tourists inside that I appreciated the true surrealistic nature of the place. There was Crocodile Harry, a shadow of his former self if the myriad photos of him as a crocodile hunter up north were any indication. The legends surrounding this man suggested he was the original Crocodile Dundee, and there were photos and newspaper clippings to corroborate it: a sturdy,

THE RED ISLAND

bearded, Stetson-hatted hunter, sometimes in a loincloth, once poking a spear in the chest of an Aboriginal companion, sometimes sitting on the three-metre reptiles that had lent him their name. But now, watching us file through his domicile, he looked as lifeless and leathery as Tutankhamen. He didn't look drunk as our guide had warned (although another man sitting at his table was comatose, his forehead resting peacefully on the laminex between a beer bottle and an empty glass). And he spoke only once, to answer a question our guide asked. Carved into convex sections of his dugout walls were sculptures of busty women. His bed had been custom built by a Japanese girl who had stayed for a while. All over the ceiling and walls were scribbled the signatures and addresses of female visitors. When our guide asked him how many names there were, he mumbled, 'Three thousand, nine hundred and ninety-nine and a half.'

Crocodile Harry's indifference impressed me. And so did his dugout. Australia was culturally diverse, even outside its cities; and that to me was its greatest strength. But it struck me that Crocodile Harry came as close as anybody to personifying the national spirit. Perhaps it was his singularity, or his willingness to live in a hole in the ground as long as he could call it his own.

The guide led us outside to show us the tattered remains of the props from *Ground Zero*, a movie that had also exploited the cataclysmic atmosphere of Crocodile Harry's dugout. Then we were off again in the mini bus to the Breakaways, a rock formation which was featured in both movies, as well as in the Australian cult hit, *Priscilla, Queen of the Desert*. It offered a stark clifftop view of the desert that rolled away towards Oodnadatta. It was a sobering sight, an expanse of incomparable land that looked as if it had been flayed.

We went down to the plain, and our guide stopped the mini bus on a lonely stretch of road. 'They reckon the centre of Australia used to be an inland sea,' he said. 'Climb out here for a while, have a look around, and see what yer reckon.'

While the tourists followed the guide across a rocky piece of ground and began to fossick where he suggested, I hurried back along the dirt road until I was a long way from the bus. I wanted to experience what it would be like to be alone out here. The air was hot but not unbearable; the scenery was astonishing. I left the road and walked across the brittle surface, towards a remote pale mesa. What intimidated me was the silence, which encircled me and pressed against my head. It was physical, almost predatory, and I felt compelled to look back to make sure the others had not gone without me. Seeing them in the distance, nonchalantly picking at the ground, reassured me. I continued towards the far-off mesa. At my feet were fossils from the sea.

Adelaide was known as the city of churches and, although I had long ago lost my faith, I was pleased to be there. It seemed civilised and sophisticated. The people in the streets seemed ordinary. I felt at home. I strolled around admiring its elegant stone buildings. I sat on the lawn by the pretty Torrens River in spring sunshine. I loitered in bookshops. And in Rundle Mall I ran into someone I knew.

Margarite was a socialist. I had got to know her when she lived in Melbourne through an interest we shared in Latin American politics. When I first heard she had moved to Adelaide, I had assumed it was on her party's instructions, but now she told me it was because her father was ill. I figured she was still in the party since she was trying to sell its broadsheet in Rundle Mall. She asked me what I was doing in Adelaide.

'Investigating the role of the rotary clothes hoist in Australian culture.'

'Oh, yeah. That enduring symbol of female oppression.'

THE RED ISLAND

'How do you figure that?'

'Women are still the ones who do the fucking washing.'

'Generally speaking. So I guess you refuse to use one.'

'Spot on, comrade,' she said, grinning. 'I use a laundromat.'

The Hare Krishna in their pale orange robes came dancing along the mall. I walked around some more. I saw a Japanese tourist complaining to police about losing her bag to a thief. I ate in the evening at an Asian street festival. Then later, at the hostel where I was staying, an old American tourist asked me to point out the constellation of the Southern Cross to him. 'You know, I don't think I've ever seen it,' he said.

He followed me slowly upstairs to the rooftop, where I looked in vain away to the south. 'It's over that way somewhere,' I said. 'But the city glare is too bright. You need to go into the outback.'

'I'm going to Coober Pedy tomorrow,' he said.

I rang my mother, and asked her if she would meet my coach just over the Victorian border at Horsham, 160 kilometres from Portland where she lived. 'Of course, I'll pick you up, darlin'!' she said. 'Just tell me what time.'

The coach left at dawn, wound out through the gentle Adelaide hills and on to Murray Bridge, where I crossed the Murray River for the second time since leaving Melbourne. Its water was brown and sluggish, a huge river weighted with silt and debris as it neared the sea. There were eucalypts and willows along its banks, but the land beyond was flat and uninspiring, with solitary trees as dead as statues. I dozed, half-thinking about my mother, Pat, whose struggle through her own life had made mine easy.

When we reached Horsham, she was standing on the footpath with another old woman, dressed in a neat slack suit. She squinted at the coach through her pale-framed glasses but could not see me. With her grey hair recently

lonely road home

permed, her face made up to cover sun spots, and her shoulders showing signs of a stoop, she looked rather frail and vulnerable. I felt guilty. 'I shouldn't have asked you to do this,' I said, kissing her cheek. 'It would have been just as easy for me to hitch.'

'It's no trouble, darlin',' she insisted. 'What would I be doing instead? Washing me socks and underwear.' She asked me if I remembered Jessie, one of the women she played bowls with. 'Jessie insisted on coming to keep me company. She forgets I travel down to Rhonnie's on me own all the time. That's twice as far as this.' My sister, Rhonda, lived on the coast near Geelong, three hours from Portland.

Jessie rolled her eyes as if to say, 'We've been through all of this before.' She had emphysema and spent a lot of time in hospital. Her bowling days were over. Accompanying Pat as far as Horsham must have been quite an ordeal for her.

'Thanks Jessie,' I said.

We had sandwiches and a cup of tea by a river before we headed off.

But instead of south, we headed west along the Wimmera Highway, with me at the wheel and Pat next to me looking pensively at the countryside. Away to the left were the Grampians, the last fragment of the Great Dividing Range, rising from a green plain. We were heading for a place where my mother and I used to live.

Some time after we left Brisbane, we lived on a property called Koijak near the little town of Apsley, a sheep station owned by Sir Magnus Cormack, President of the Australian Senate. My mother kept the homestead in order, cooked for the shearers and for Sir Magnus on his monthly visits. Occasionally, when he had guests staying, she prepared dinner which was held in an opulent dining room. And Sir Magnus would compliment her, declaring she made the best French omelettes in the world.

I was six and happy to be living on a farm. I liked to

THE RED ISLAND

climb into the old walnut trees behind the homestead, or walk alone down the low-lying land we used to call 'the swamp' that was surrounded by sprawling gum trees. I liked the solitude. I went to school in Apsley and had my friends, but I was glad to leave them and return home each day. School holidays on the farm were the happiest time of my young life.

A few things had changed in Apsley in our forty-year absence, although not a great deal. A section of the primary school I had attended had been pulled down. A couple of the old stores were still standing, but empty. I couldn't find the small park I used to play in after school while waiting for my mother to pick me up.

It took us a few false turns before we found Koijak at the end of a lonely lane. It had a new entrance, a concrete arch set in stone. Sir Magnus had subdivided the sheep station before he sold it, and the section that still bore its name was now a stud cattle property. The front paddock was empty, the manager's cottage and the homestead still standing at opposite ends. I drove slowly along its powdery track, searching for things to recognise. The swamp seemed closer to the homestead than it used to be.

I stopped the car on the track before the homestead, unwilling to enter its yard. We looked across young grass to the broad white building, with its decorative window shutters and corrugated-iron roof. The elaborate gardens were gone, replaced by lawn. The fibro-cement sheet extension at one end of the domestic quarters, which had been my bedroom, was still there. 'It looks shabbier than what I remember,' I said.

'They probably don't have the money old Cormack had,' Pat said. 'Or at least her ladyship. She was the one with the money.'

'It's not that shabby that I wouldn't live in it,' Jessie muttered.

lonely road home

I drove down some back roads through hilly country to Portland. The cattle were up to their bellies in fresh spring grass. It was odd to be travelling through green undulating countryside after months of red soil and distant horizons. I liked the winding road, the views across hilltops that disappeared after a moment, the changes. It kept me alert and interested. The colour of everything was intense and sombre. The paddocks were full of flighty lambs.

As we neared Portland, the land flattened again and the gum trees became straight and spindly. 'What are you getting old Frank for tea?' Pat asked Jessie, her thoughts shifting to domestic duties as she neared home.

Jessie had been married for forty-odd years. 'Hot tongue and cold shoulder,' she wheezed.

———

Portland was the oldest established settlement in Victoria. Its founders, the Henty brothers, came from Tasmania and expropriated as much land as they needed for their sheep. They built high walls topped with broken glass around their homesteads to protect them from the natives. The town was perched on white cliffs around a bay in the south-west of the state. When I was a child there in the last years of primary school, it was a seaside resort and port. Old timber piers stretched out into the harbour, one with a railway and a lever-operated trolley that I used to ride to the storage sheds over the sea. There were Edwardian sea baths with changing rooms and a kiosk, and crumbling breakwaters whose rocks were the hideaway of conger eels. In the town there were old bluestone buildings and the streets ran between rows of Norfolk pines. At various stages, decisions were made to transform Portland into a modern port. Somehow that entailed removing the town's historic charm. Some of the oldest buildings in Victoria were demolished so

THE RED ISLAND

that a bland brick civic centre and shire offices could be built on their site. Pines were taken out to widen the streets. The old piers and baths were dismantled beam by beam.

Up until the late sixties, holidaying families from the hinterland would triple Portland's population in the summer months. Henty Beach, with its row of colourful bathers' huts, art deco changing rooms, swings and slides and children's pantomimes, was always crowded. An old woman who wore a broad straw hat, a frock that never suited her muscular body, with a bulging leather money pouch around her sturdy waist, ran a popular paddleboat and trampoline business like a sergeant major. The shallows were full of whooping children. On the foreshore, or rather on vacant land at the end of a shunting yard at the railway station, a carnival of sideshows, shooting galleries, ferris wheels and wheels of fortune operated.

After we dropped Jessie off and went home, I told Pat I needed to stretch my legs. I went to the beach, which, except for a gathering of idle gulls, was deserted. I left the beach, crossed a canal and entered the port, first to the fishing fleet along the old breakwater and then to view the land reclamation that extended from here across the K.S. Anderson wharf, which had all been deep water when I was young. The conger eels had lost their sanctuary. The cliffs at Battery Point were no longer by the sea.

I enjoyed the stench of trawlers. It was unambiguous and potent. It signalled hard work and honest endeavour, the smell that puts meals on tables. My father, Denny, had worked in Portland after he stopped selling clothes hoists, but as a wharfie, loading wheat and meat into the hulls of ships on sixteen or twenty-four hour shifts. Later, he helped build a fish factory near the trawlers' wharf, until the scaffolding he was on collapsed and he crushed several discs in his spine.

Pat had dinner ready when I returned: lamb chops, mashed potatoes and peas. I sat at one end of the small table

lonely road home

in her kitchenette, and ate while she chatted about what had been happening to her in Portland. I half-listened, as I always did, to what she said, stories about her bowling club or people whose names meant nothing to me.

Her living room was a photo gallery and a gallery of bowling trophies. Six generations were represented in the photos, from her grandparents to her great-grandchildren. There was her wedding photo, when she and Denny were in their twenties, half my age. Pat looked sweet and happy, while Denny looked rather awkward and dazed, as if the significance of the occasion had just occurred to him. Nearby was another of my younger sister's wedding. And Denny was in it too, giving away the bride a year or so after losing half his stomach to cancer, a diminished figure with a look of happy incredulity on his gaunt face. His life to that point had been a maelstrom and would continue with the same flurry for another ten years. But this snap of Denny smiling like someone who was the sole survivor of a national catastrophe was nearest the image of him I carried in my head.

I spent a few days in Portland. I walked around town, searching out my old haunts. The Star Theatre where I worked for five years as a lolly boy was now a cinematheque and shopping complex. I passed the old bluestone Anglican church where I had been an altar boy, and my sister had been married, and Denny had had his funeral. I went out to the housing commission estate in West Portland where I had lived in the mid-sixties. The house had been repainted and bushes I had planted in the front yard were fully grown. But the street looked the same. It was here, with my mate Steve, that I had first planned to travel Australia, lounging in my room, pubescent and virginal, dreaming of adventure.

I went with Pat to a magnificent beach at Bridgewater Bay. I was glad it wasn't in the tourist guidebooks; its obscurity kept it relatively pristine. It extended for miles in an

THE RED ISLAND

unbroken sweep between Cape Nelson and Cape Bridgewater, a broad stretch of white sand against sandy cliffs. There were some houses on the hills behind the beach, but the land that rose towards Cape Bridgewater was pasture, a great emerald bulge sheltering the shore that eventually folded down to granite cliffs towering a hundred metres or more above the sea.

In winter this beach was deserted. I was fond of walking for hours along it, alone, wrapped in a coat, the sea spray dense enough to obscure the lighthouse at Cape Nelson, and an icy gale to remind me that I was still alive. Now, in spring, I could see a couple of figures close to the water, and three surfers sat on their boards in black wetsuits, waiting for the next swell to thrust them towards the shore. I walked with Pat, happy to be there and to be with her.

And before I left for Melbourne, I did something I hadn't done in ten years. I went to see Denny's grave. He had died of cancer in the early eighties. And every month since, Pat had visited the bleak Portland cemetery on a sandy hill south of the town. She kept the weeds down, touched up the gold lettering when it began to flake. She bought a posy of flowers each visit. 'He didn't have much luck in life,' I said.

'He didn't, Graeme. That's for sure.' She stood for a while by his headstone, then checked the graves of her father, eldest brother and brother-in-law nearby.

It was a five-hour trip home: by bus across the Eumerella shore, past Port Fairy, a lovely seaside resort, and through the potato and onion fields of Killarney and Koroit to Warrnambool, where I caught a train to Melbourne. The train was stifling and half-empty. Its passengers found seats as far away from others as possible. I read, but looked up at the Stony Rises, a geological oddity with volcanic origins

212

lonely road home

where convicts last century had been forced to build stone fences as they cleared the land for farming. I raised an eyebrow when we stopped at Geelong, a port city an hour south of Melbourne. I didn't put my book down until we were crossing thistle fields near the Altona petro-chemical plants on the outskirts of the city. When we passed through the shabby suburb of Footscray I caught a glimpse of the building near the Maribyrnong River where I had taught English to migrants before this journey began. And I remembered a conversation I'd had with a Chinese student just before I left:

'I hear this word "orgy", and I don't know what it means. I hear it everywhere.'

'You do?'

'Yes, "orgy".'

'It's when several people have sex together. Understand?'

'I understand your words, but don't understand.'

'Look, give me an example of where you've heard it. Put it in a sentence.'

'I hear it on TV. Like when they call a Ford a good orgy car.'

'An orgy car? Oh, you mean Aussie! A good Aussie car!'

'Ah, yes! Orgy! That's it, an orgy car. What's it mean?'

'It means Australian. It's short for Australian.'

It reminded me of Robert Hughes' account of the convicts' first night at Sydney Cove. To call us 'orgies' seemed definitive enough. I looked at the passengers around me. None was Chinese, Vietnamese, Somalian, Latin American, or Bosnian. They had the bland faces of fifth-generation Australians, Western District faces, probably of Irish stock. Orgies through and through. None of them looked happy. But that was the effect arriving in Melbourne could have on country folk. I looked through the window and saw the tall grey skyscrapers huddled on the far side of Victoria Docks. Home, I thought, and I'm the only one on this train who's smiling. When the train stopped at Spencer

THE RED ISLAND

Street Station, I took a suburban train the last kilometre to Flinders Street. And I walked out under the clocks to see the piper in his wheelchair and the school children loitering in fashionable rap gear and the green trams rumbling along Swanston Walk.

I was back in my city but my journey wasn't over. Tasmania beckoned, the smallest Australian state. I borrowed Tania's car and took a ferry overnight to Devonport. By nine o'clock I had disembarked and, after a quick look around the quiet town, headed south through fertile farmland. There was no coastal plain to speak of: Tasmania was hilly right to the shore. And behind the hills, irregular rock pinnacles pierced an unexpected blue sky.

Launceston was at the top of an estuary called the Tamar River, fifty kilometres from the coast. It was the city where my mother and father met, where they married and my sisters and I were born, a lovely place tumbling down the sides of hills into the estuary valley, with steep streets, elegant timber houses, and impressive old city buildings. I stayed in a motel that had been cleverly built in an old stone quarry, with all the amenities I used to dream about on my trip around the mainland. I drove around Launceston, finding the address where we had lived with my grandmother. The old place had been demolished to build a studio for the Australian Broadcasting Commission. I remembered the park opposite where I used to collect acorns, and a swing which once split my eye.

Afterwards I went for a walk along a path cut into the mossy wall of the Cataract Gorge, as far as a swinging bridge across First Basin. When my mother came to Launceston just after the war and met Denny, he showed her the gorge, which had a series of basins joined by cataracts.

lonely road home

He used to swim down them to impress her. And once he chased a duck around the icy water of First Basin until it was exhausted and he was able to capture it. That was an anecdote she was fond of recounting when she wanted to remember the young man she had fallen in love with.

The next day I travelled down the wild east coast and stopped for lunch at Bicheno whose lovely beach, between oblique slabs of granite, was occupied by a host of hymn-singing, evangelical Christians. I visited Freycinet National Park and hiked over its pink granite mountains to Wineglass Bay. Late in the afternoon I went up to a lighthouse on Cape Tourville, one of a group of stark mountains that dropped into the sea. A French sailor Louis Freycinet passed this way in the eighteenth century, naming every salient rock in sight after his crew—Freycinet, Tourville, Forestier, Degerando, Sonnerat, Ile des Phoques, Faure, Fleurieu—crude pinnacles and promontories and dangerous projections from the sea.

Hobart surprised me. Its setting on the wide Derwent River, beneath Mount Wellington and Mount Nelson, rivalled Sydney's. Indeed, the proximity of the mountains and the brooding weather that rolled off the slopes gave it a dramatic aspect the tiny hills and sunshine in Sydney could never offer. And because it had escaped much of the progress of the mainland capitals, its early Georgian architecture, some of it in pink granite from Coles Bay near Freycinet, still influenced the character of the city. Small enough to walk around, I traipsed its cold streets and walked along the waterfront which had barely changed since the early 1800s.

In Tasmania it was possible to get anywhere there were roads within a day. The roads were usually narrow and

THE RED ISLAND

winding, which made driving tiring, but the views at every turn were adequate compensation. One day I travelled into south-west Tasmania to see the flooded Lake Pedder and a remarkable dam across a chasm on the Gordon River. The countryside here was as wild as any I had seen in the world: crinkled folds of mountains all around, treacherous ravines, forest so dense in places that individual plants were difficult to discern. Where paths had been cut into the forest by national park rangers, the canopy absorbed most of the light. Beneath it was silent and spooky. Strange gangly horizontal trees grew. A sodden blanket of moss carpeted the forest floor.

On another occasion I drove to the west coast, over the central highlands, past Lake St Clair at the southern end of the Overland walking track to Cradle Mountain, and through the denuded hills around Queenstown, where the landscape was as desolate as what I'd seen around Coober Pedy. Queenstown had been a copper mine settlement, and the forest had disappeared into its smelter furnaces. I stopped at Strahan, a pretty fishing village that had ironically enjoyed a eco-tourist boom since its residents had publicly fought with greenies trying to protect the region from the timber and power industries. Here I took a cruise along Macquarie Harbour, an inlet that penetrated thirty kilometres into the mountainous terrain, past lonely Sarah Island, Tasmania's first brutal penal settlement, to where the harbour narrowed and became the Gordon River. The cruiser slowed and crept up the river, which was brown with tannin leached from the high plains' button grass, until it stopped at a jetty that led to a designated walkway into rainforest. I disembarked and followed the crowd to view a Huon pine—a hoary giant, split and gnarled, and dressed in mossy garb— that was on this earth before the birth of Christ.

Hobart was overcast all the time I was there. But the locals were always cheerful. It was strange to be in an

lonely road home

Australian city where the racial mixture seemed so straight-forward. Tasmania had largely missed out on the influx of recent migrants that made other states, particularly their capitals, places of great diversity. It seemed like the land of my youth, when Anglo culture went unquestioned and the only migrants to be seen ran restaurants.

In other unrelated ways this impression prevailed. The pleasantness of people you encountered in shops and cafes seemed quaintly old fashioned. Children were often left alone, outside supermarkets on benches or in prams, while their mothers shopped. There was an old-fashioned trusting culture in Tasmania that made it seem rather innocent.

That was soon to change forever. But on a sunny day, four months before the massacre, I went to Port Arthur, smiling at my good fortune with the weather.

The penal settlement was on the Tasman Peninsula an hour to the east of Hobart. Like the rest of Tasmania, the peninsula had a desolate beauty that must have seemed cruel to the wretched prisoners who had been incarcerated here. Once you crossed Eaglehawk Neck, the narrowest of land bridges that had been guarded by savage dogs in the days of the penal settlement, a sensation of doom hung over the land. It pervaded the listless forest and rolled like fog across the calm sea.

The dismal ruins of the penal settlement—the shells of its penitentiary, church and hospital, parts of the military compound, the model prison, the lunatic asylum and the commandant's house—overlooked a lonely harbour, sur-rounded by forested hills. It was hard to imagine what went through the minds of the hapless convicts who were brought to Port Arthur, but each one must have been convinced they were arriving at the end of the earth.

THE RED ISLAND

The weather turned. It poured all night, and in the morning it was still showery. The clouds were low and gnarled. I wanted to go as far south as I could, to the southernmost tip of Australia if possible, which seemed a fitting way to finish my journey.

I figured from my map I could drive as far as Cockle Creek.

I took the highway past Mount Nelson to Kingston. The hills were hidden in mist and the road was wet and treacherous. I wanted to detour down the coastal road to Oyster Cove to see the place, decreed unfit for convicts, where a handful of Aboriginals, the only survivors of Governor Arthur's 'Black Line' genocidal dragnet, had been held captive after 1856. But the weather was deteriorating, so I kept to the highway. I passed through Huonville and followed the estuary of the Huon River south. There were marshes along its banks and dark water.

All over Tasmania I had seen fields of opium poppies, cultivated under government supervision. Now I noticed apple orchards. I crossed some vivid green farmland. With each elevation in the road, I was travelling in clouds. Rain set in and reduced my visibility, slowing me, fraying my nerves. When I reached the seaside village of Dover, I parked by the shore to rest. A fishing boat was returning to the harbour. Through listless rain I watched a lone crewman in yellow waterproofs gaff its moorings from the sea, climb into a tiny dinghy, and row slowly ashore.

I went further south, through Southport and Lune River. When the bitumen ended, I wondered whether to continue. The dirt road was gleaming in the wet, but there were no visible furrows from other vehicles to indicate its condition. I was determined to go as far as possible. I followed the greasy road through a forest limp with rain, until I was in sight of Recherche Bay. A few holiday huts here were marked on the map as Catamaran. At the southern

lonely road home

tip of the bay was Cockle Creek.

The road had deteriorated into a series of watery pot-holes. Mist obscured the bay and the final hills to the open sea. I drove on, dodging the worst of the potholes until it seemed unwise to continue. There were huts, caravans and sodden tents set amongst sandy mounds, and a few substantial bungalows. Dinghies were moored just offshore. There was not a human to be seen.

'I suppose this is it,' I muttered to myself.

Then, on a vacant block between the track and the sea, I saw a remarkable sight. There were no houses nearby, just this patch of lawn with a stack of bricks to one side. In the middle of the block was a rusting old rotary clothes hoist, the sort my father used to sell.

More quality non-fiction from
The Text Publishing Company

BEYOND TIJUANA:
A JOURNEY THROUGH LATIN AMERICA
Graeme Sparkes

A travel book of great clarity and grace, written with an eagle
eye for irresistible detail: the majestic extremities of the
landscape, the grubby hotels, the antiquity of the culture,
the endemic poverty, and the extraordinary people Sparkes
meets on the road.

'A quirky and generous book ... Sparkes captures the flavours,
the heat, the exhaustion and the endless fascination
of cultures so different from his own.' *Age*

224pp, paperback, rrp $16.95 ISBN 1 875847 19 7

ON THE LOOSE
John Button

A funny and charming account of life after
politics by the retired Labor senator. Button writes hilariously
about everything under the sun, from Christmas shopping
to minding the dog, from the rights of smokers to the joys of
jogging—and muses on the republican debate, political
correctness and parliamentary language. He globetrots to
Hong Kong, Hanoi, New York and Ballarat, casting a
keen eye over the locals wherever he goes.

224pp, paperback, rrp $16.95 ISBN 1 875847 35 9

1788
Watkin Tench
Edited by Tim Flannery

Tench, a humble captain-lieutenant of the marines, arrived
on the First Fleet and, with his characteristic understanding,
humanity and eye for detail, recorded the first few years of
European settlement. A classic, lovingly edited by Tim
Flannery, author of the best-selling *The Future Eaters*.

'Not to have read Watkin Tench is not to know early
Australia. An eye that noticed everything, a young man's
verve, a sly wit, an elegant prose style—all brought to bear
on an unimagined place and a very strange micro-society.
This is the most readable classic of early Australian history.'
Robert Hughes

288pp, paperback, rrp $16.95 ISBN 1 875847 27 8

TRUE STORIES: SELECTED NON-FICTION
Helen Garner

Helen Garner visits the morgue, and goes cruising
on a Russian ship. She sees women giving birth, and gets
the sack for teaching her students about sex.
She attends a school dance and a gun show.
True Stories spans twenty-five years of work by one
of Australia's greatest writers.

'Helen Garner writes the best sentences in Australia.'
Ed Campion, *Bulletin*

256pp, paperback, rrp $19.95 ISBN 1 875847 24 3